D1477149

WOOD GREEN
PAST

Acknowledgements

I would firstly like to thank my many colleagues in the Hornsey Historical Society for their interest and encouragement since undertaking this work. Special thanks are due to Joan Schwitzer and Ken Gay for taking the trouble to read the draft manuscript and for their helpful and constructive comments.

The material for this book has resulted from many visits to archives and musea. I would like to particularly thank Rita Read, of Haringey's Bruce Castle Museum, for her valued help extending over several years, and Kevin Lincoln, of Haringey Property Services, for dealing so obligingly with my many enquiries. Also, my thanks to the staff at the London Metropolitan Archives, the Guildhall Library, the British Library and Graham Dalling of Enfield Libraries. Mention must also be made of those Wood Green residents and others whose memories and anecdotes have been appreciated. Special thanks also to Jacqueline Guyatt and Ken Barker for access to material relating to Westbury House and South's Potteries respectively.

I also wish to record my appreciation of the use of the Hornsey Historical Society Archives and in particular for access to the research notes and texts of the late Cecil J. Harris, a fellow local historian, from whose detailed work on Ducketts Manor and Farm and other subjects I have drawn freely.

Albert Pinching

The Illustrations

We are grateful to the following for permission to use illustrations.

Ken Barker: 23, 98, 99, 100, 101
N. Beecham: 96
Capital and Regional Properties: 139, 140
Cinema Theatre Association: 191
Dean and Chapter of St Paul's Cathedral (deposit at Guildhall Library MS 18798): 4
David Dell: 10, 21, 45, 54, 69, 88, 114, 127, 187
Keith Fawkes-Underwood: 3
Peter Garland: 12, 30
Hugh Garnsworthy: 67, 71, 76
Ken Gay: 25, 106
Tony Gay: 170
Brenda Griffith-Williams 183
Guildhall Library, City of London: 5, 29
Jacqueline Guyatt: 36, 37
Hackney Archives: 14
London Borough of Haringey, Bruce Castle Museum: 6, 50, 51, 52, 53, 57, 58, 59, 60, 61, 62, 63, 64, 65, 66, 68, 8, 11, 16, 17, 18, 22, 24, 26, 27, 28, 31, 32, 33, 39, 43, 46, 72, 73, 77, 78, 79, 80, 82, 83, 84, 92, 103, 107, 108, 117, 119, 120, 122, 124, 125, 126, 129, 132, 134, 135, 136, 137, 141, 142, 143, 145, 147, 149, 151, 153, 154, 155, 156, 157, 159, 160, 161, 162, 163, 164, 165, 166, 171, 172, 173, 174, 176, 179, 181, 182, 189, 190, 192, 193
John B. Parkes: 130
Historical Publications Ltd: 15, 109, 115, 186
Hornsey Historical Society: 104, 175
Hornsey Journal: 168, 169
National Monuments Record: 7, 70, 91
North Middlesex Photographic Society: 19
Albert Pinching: 1, 2, 9, 13, 20, 34, 38, 40, 41, 44, 48, 49, 55, 56, 74, 75, 81, 85, 89, 90, 93, 94, 95, 97, 102, 105, 110, 111, 112, 113, 116, 118, 121, 123, 131, 133, 138, 144, 150, 152, 158, 177, 178, 180, 184, 185, 188
Providence Convent: 42, 86
Society of Friends: 35
Malcolm Stokes: 148
D.A. Thompson: 146
Peter Watson: 47

First published 2000 by Historical Publications Ltd
32 Ellington Street, London N7 8PL (Tel: 020 7607 1628)
© **Albert Pinching**

ISBN 0 948667 64 8
British Library Cataloguing-in-Publication Data
A catalogue record for this book is available from the British Library
Typeset in Palatino by Historical Publications Ltd
Reproduction by G & J Graphics, London EC2
Printed in Zaragoza, Spain, by Edelvives

WOOD GREEN PAST

Albert Pinching

HISTORICAL PUBLICATIONS

Introduction

Soon after coming to live in Wood Green 25 years ago I became a member of a residents' group. This in turn led to involvement in a Conservation Area Committee and the Alexandra Palace Consultative Committee and an increased awareness of the history of the area. However, at that time there was little published on the history of Wood Green. Coverage in the *Victoria County History: Middlesex*, Vol.V had to be extracted from the chapter on Tottenham but it was limited on the people and places in my own locality.

This does not mean that Wood Green had been ignored by historians and commentators. William Bedwell, Vicar of Tottenham (1607-1632), was the first historian of Tottenham with his *A Briefe Description of the Towne of Tottenham Highcrosse in Middlesex* (1631) in which he makes reference to Wood Green. He was followed by Lysons in *Environs of London* (1796, 1811) but it was not until Robinson's *History and Antiquities of Tottenham* (1840) that more detailed descriptions of Wood Green emerged. Fisk's *History of Tottenham* (1st edn 1913, 2nd edn 1923) reviewed much of the earlier work reinforced with his own observations on later developments including those in Wood Green. Following the creation of Wood Green Urban District Council a series of *Wood Green Guides* appeared. These, with contributions by the Borough Librarian, W.G. Peplow, together with Council publications like the *Town Crier* during the 1960s, helped to fill in some of the gaps in Wood Green's past.

Directories and gazetteers also provided information on the growth of neighbourhoods, trades and amenities. Other sources of information are the descriptions by commentators on north London suburbs. Edward Walford in *Greater London* (1883) described a rural scene before full-scale urbanisation. Perhaps the lengthiest description of Wood Green and Bowes Park was that of Thomas Burke in his *Outer Circle* (1921), who devoted a chapter to each with his very personalised views. Of Wood Green, Burke said:

> Wood Green is one of the few London suburbs that lack recorded history. Pepys never saw it. Queen Elizabeth did not sleep there. Sir Walter Besant is silent about it. It is off the main North Road, and has no old taverns or churches. I find no word of it in literature. It has been ignored by the novelist, the essayist, and the topographist.

These words were written in 1921, and he must have missed the official guide of 1910. Later commentators such as Briggs in *Middlesex: Old and New* (1934) and Robbins in *Middlesex* (1953) were also somewhat dismissive of Wood Green and of Alexandra Palace in particular. There is still no definitive history, but I hope the present volume will go some way towards that objective.

Recent illustrated books such as *In Times Past* (1991) and *Tottenham, Hornsey and Wood Green* (1998) did much to provide a visual insight into Wood Green's past.

My own researches began with tracing the history of some of the early Wood Green estates, the houses and their occupants. The results of some of these studies were published in *People and Places; Lost Estates of Highgate, Hornsey and Wood Green* (1996) and in subsequent issues of the *Hornsey Historical Society Bulletin* (1997, 1998, 1999). A contribution to the Hornsey Historical Society's series of walks entitled *Discovering Old Wood Green: A Walk* was published in 1998.

In this new book I have attempted to present the story of Wood Green as a whole with illustrations, many of which have not been previously published between hard covers.

Wood Green began as a hamlet during the Middle Ages once surrounded by the forest of Middlesex. Its location alongside an important highway encouraged its development as did the conversion of forest into farmland during the 17th and 18th centuries. Growth accelerated with the railways in the mid-19th century and the creation of the Alexandra Park and Palace, after which it was transformed into a London suburb. It became a parish in its own right in 1866, separated administratively from Tottenham in 1888, became an Urban District in 1894 and progressed to full Borough status in 1933.

The book concentrates on the area covered by the former Urban District and Borough of Wood Green up to its amalgamation into the London Borough of Haringey in 1965. Subsequent developments are briefly described in a postscript.

Finally, a plea. Much of the source material used in this book was gleaned from the Borough of Haringey's Bruce Castle Museum and from the Borough Engineer's archives. This book would have been impossible without this information. I therefore appeal to Haringey Council, and other local authorities, to ensure the upkeep, security and accessibility of such invaluable sources for the benefit of future generations.

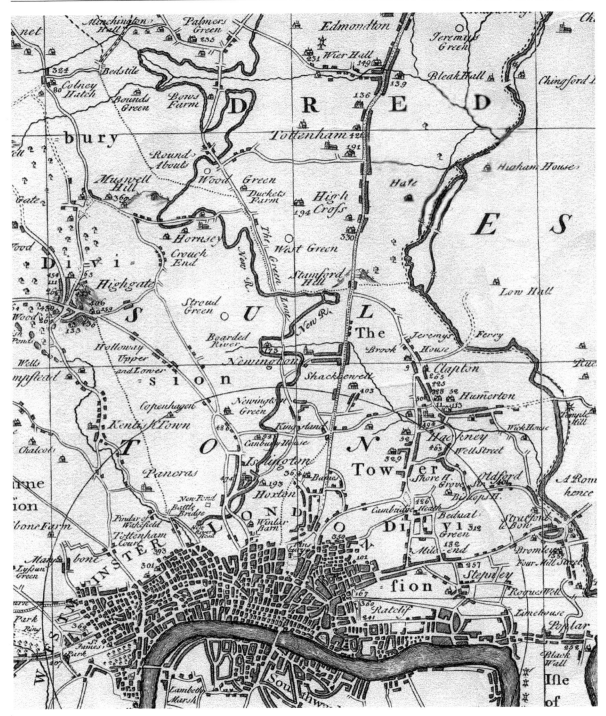

1. *Extract from John Warburton's 'Map of the City of London and Middlesex', 1749. It shows the route of Green Lanes from Newington Green to Wood Green and beyond.*

Wood Green Defined

Today, the district of Wood Green, once defined by the former municipal borough of the same name, is a central part of the London Borough of Haringey and consists of about 1600 acres. It includes the whole of the N22 and parts of the N8, N10, N11 and N17 postal districts and encompasses the Alexandra, Bowes Park, Woodside, Noel Park, and parts of the Muswell Hill and White Hart Lane electoral wards.

The heart of the area was once the green, or common. By the early 16th century the name Wood Green applied to an ecclesiastical ward covering the western half of the parish of Tottenham which once extended from the parish of Edmonton to the north, Stoke Newington to the south, and included what are now the districts of Harringay and West Green; on the west and south-west it was bounded by the parish of Hornsey. The Wood Green ward remained an entity for parish administration for over three centuries.

With the formation of the Tottenham Local Board of Health in 1850, the Wood Green ward became an area of civic administration until the creation of the Wood Green Local Board of Health and its separation from Tottenham in 1888. At this time the southern districts of Harringay and West Green remained part of Tottenham. The earlier definition of the Wood Green ward, however, remained intact for electoral purposes into the 20th century.

The district lies both sides of Wood Green High Road which runs north-south from Turnpike Lane to Palmers Green as part of Green Lanes. The northern boundaries of the civic entity of Wood Green, from Local Board, through Urban District Council to Borough Council, remained essentially unchanged and from 1888 its southern boundary has been defined by Turnpike Lane and Westbury Avenue.

This story of Wood Green concentrates on the area of the former municipal borough but also makes reference to the areas in the south-east once part of the old ecclesiastical ward.

To the south and east, towards the Lea Valley, the land is flat. To the north-west the land rises, reaching 200 feet at Bounds Green, and to the south-west it rises towards Muswell Hill and Highgate, with Alexandra Palace at 300 feet.

2. *Extract from John Cary's map of Middlesex, 1793.*

RIVERS

The area is crossed by four natural watercourses, all now mostly culverted. The Muswell Stream rises from the 'Mus well' or 'Mossy Well' now located beneath no. 40 Muswell Road, and flows north-east via Albert Road to the High Road, close to Woodside Park, and then north to join Pymmes Brook in Palmers Green. The Moselle also rises on the western slopes and flows through Hornsey and then north-east under Shopping City and Noel Park and Broadwater Farm estates, eventually joining the Lea. An open stretch of the Moselle can still be seen in Lordship Lane Recreation Ground. The Stonebridge Brook traverses the southern end of the district, flowing east from the vicinity of Hornsey Town Hall, along Hornsey Vale and Effingham Road, under Green Lanes at St Ann's Road and on to Seven Sisters Road to reach the Lea at Markfield Park. A shorter stream, Coppetts Brook, rises near Coldfall Wood and flows north to join Bounds Green Brook which flows across the north-west corner of the area to join Pymmes Brook. These watercourses often formed estate boundaries.

The area is also crossed north to south by the man-made New River, which now flows in a tunnel replacing its once meandering route through Wood Green. This river, created in the 17th century, had an impact on development.

Early History

ORIGINS

The name Wood Green conjures up a rural and sylvan scene, as indeed it once was. It derives from *'woodlegh'* or *'woodlea'* (of Saxon origin) meaning meadow or open ground in or near the wood, in this case Tottenham Wood, the site of today's Alexandra Park.

In prehistoric times large tracts of dense forest, principally oak, ash and beech covered Middlesex. Clearings or 'greens' existed naturally or were made by the early occupants, possibly the ancient British tribes but most likely the Anglo-Saxons. These early occupants probably made the first track-ways and paths through the forest.

An ancient track, today's Green Lanes, ran north from London towards Enfield and Hertford, connecting several greens lying between today's Manor House and Palmers Green, including Wood Green, once known as Woodleigh or Tottenham Wode Green.

THE ROMANS

At the time of Julius Ceasar's first expeditions to Britain in 55 and 54 BC the area north of the Thames, including today's Hertfordshire, Buckinghamshire and Middlesex, was the home of the Catuvellauni and Trinovantes, ancient British tribes. Under the leadership of Cassivellaunus, the Britons with their chariots, cavalry and knowledge of the forest harassed the Roman advance but were eventually subdued at their stronghold at Wheathampstead, in Hertfordshire, and a treaty made with Caesar.

The subsequent invasion of Britain initiated in AD 43 by Emperor Claudius saw rapid colonisation of England with the present Home Counties becoming part of the province of Britannia Superior in the 3rd century, and of Maxima Ceasarensis in the 4th, ruled from London. During their occupation the Romans constructed two major roads through the Middlesex forest: Watling Street to St Albans and Ermine Street running more or less due north through Tottenham parallel to the River Lea.

Local evidence of Roman presence is limited to a poujard, or small dagger, unearthed in the Bounds Green area in 1936, a teradrachma coin minted in Alexandria in AD 284 found on the site of Devonshire Hill School in 1945 and a coin also of the Diocletian period (AD 284-305) found in Alexandra Park.

3. *Roman dagger or poujard found at Bounds Green in 1936.*

THE SAXONS

When the Romans ended their occupation early in the 5th century, the Saxons invaded and today's Essex, Hertfordshire and Middlesex became the kingdom of the East Saxons, but by the 7th century what became Middlesex was part of the kingdom of Mercia. In the mid 9th century, Mercia, including London, fell to the Danes, but was reclaimed in 886 by King Alfred who made a treaty with the Danes. Under this the river Lea formed the boundary between Danish territory, the Danelaw, to the east and north, and Saxon territory, Wessex, to the west. The Lea later became the boundary between the counties of Essex and Middlesex which were established by the 10th century. By this time also, the county of Middlesex was divided into administrative areas known as Hundreds: Tottenham formed the southern part of the Edmonton Hundred.

Skirmishes between Saxons and Danes continued after the treaty. In 894 the Danes sailed up the Lea and established a fortress near Ware. In response, King Alfred led an army, comprising many Londoners, to rout the Danes by damming the river and stranding their ships. It is suggested that Alfred's army reached Ware by way of the trackway, Green Lanes. Alfred made further successful attacks on Danish strongholds in the Lea Valley and his son, Edward the Elder, established two fortresses at Hertford, which led in time to the English recapture of much of the Danelaw by 917. In 1016 the Danes, under Canute, laid siege to London but were subjected to surprise attack and were routed by the English king, Edmund Ironside, in the forested area to the north of London. According to the *Anglo-Saxon Chronicle* this battle took place at '*Clayhangre*', thought by some historians to be in the vicinity of Clay Hill, now Devonshire Hill, in the north-eastern extremity of our area.

Today, there is no obvious evidence of Saxon presence in the Wood Green area but they probably developed the trackways and paths in the forest, some of which survived in the form of country lanes up to modern times.

THE MANORS

Following the Norman Conquest of 1066, William I conducted a survey of his kingdom in 1086 which is recorded in the Domesday Book. There is an entry for the manor of Tottenham (*Toteham*) but there is no specific reference to Wood Green. The survey records an adult male population in Tottenham of only 66 including a priest, which indicates a total population of between 200-300. The mention of a priest suggests that a Tottenham church existed – one was certainly endowed by King David I of Scotland in 1132.

At the time of the Domesday survey the lord of the manor of Tottenham was Countess Judith, widow of Waltheof, one-time Earl of Northampton, and niece of William I. In 1254 the manor was divided into three – Bruses, Balliol and Hastings. Seven sub-manors also existed. One of these, Ducketts, was the subject of a grant in 1256 which refers to land 'in Woodlegh, Tottenham'. This appears to be the earliest surviving reference to the Wood Green area.

From the 12th century a system of government operated through several manorial courts until 1429 when a single court for all Tottenham manors was established by John Gedeney. It regulated affairs on behalf of the lord of the manor including the admission to and surrender of properties by tenants. They were known as copyhold tenants because they obtained a copy of the relevant entry in the manor court rolls.

The surviving Tottenham court rolls run from 1318 and from the latter part of the fourteenth century general descriptions of the copyhold estates and their tenants in the Wood Green area become clearer.

It has been suggested that the hospital of St Lawrence at Clayhanger, in the gift of the vicar of Tottenham, and recorded between 1229-1264, may have stood at Clay Hill (Devonshire Hill) There is, however an alternative view that the hospital was further south, in the vicinity of Hanger Lane.

DUCKETTS ESTATE

Though much of the Wood Green area was owned by the lord of the manor in medieval times, there were other estates owned freehold by individuals or by the Church. One of these was Ducketts, east of the High Road in the area of Westbury Avenue, its northern and eastern boundary defined by the Moselle river. It was one of the seven sub-manors noted above and first mentioned in 1256 when 160 acres of arable land were granted by James de Stevinton and Isabella, his wife, to a John Renger who was a clerk to Henry III. The land was subsequently granted to Laurence Duket, a City of London goldsmith, who held various other properties in Tottenham. Duket was descended from Norman knights who were part of William the Conquerer's invasion force of 1066.

Duket was involved in the tumultuous events of his time and which caused his downfall. In 1272 he was implicated in a murder for which he was pardoned only by the intervention of a nephew of Henry III. In 1284, to settle a long-standing feud between him and a powerful City administrator, John le Crepin, in which both engaged professional criminals, he eventually fought and seriously wounded Crepin in Cheapside in the City. Fearing reprisals Ducket sought sanctuary in St Mary-le-Bow Church, in Cheapside, but he was sought out by Crepin's associates and hanged from one of the windows. The perpetrators were themselves subsequently caught and hanged by the authorities. On his death Ducket's estates passed to his son, also Laurence, who became a Coroner of the County of Middlesex.

In 1360 reference was made to 'Ducketts Manor and Farm', and by 1388 a John Doget (a variation of spelling) and his wife owned the freehold of the manor and farm which then comprised 300 acres of arable land, 50 acres meadow and 40 acres woodland.

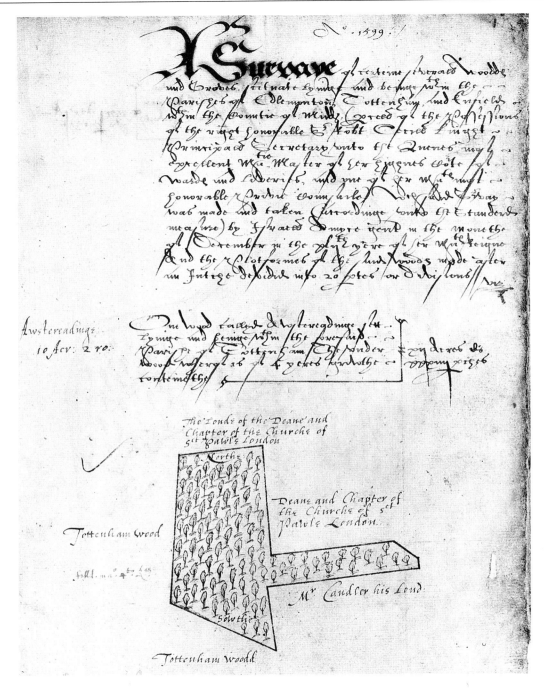

4. Plan of 'Austereadinge' by Israel Amyce dated 1599.

In 1458, the manor was bequeathed by John Sturgeon, a London merchant, to St Bartholomew's Hospital at a time when it was leased by John Watson, a brewer. In 1532, Sir John Brereton, Chaplain to Henry VIII, became master and custodian of St Bartholomew's and leased Ducketts to his brother, William, who was Chamberlain of Chester and groom of the Privy Chamber. His presence at Court seems to have given him the opportunity to commit adultery with Queen Anne (Boleyn), at a time when the king's interest was turning to Jane Seymour. Brereton's indiscretions led to his arrest, trial and execution, along with three others convicted of treason, at Tower Hill.

In 1539, the Monastery and Hospital of St Bartholemew's and all its properties, including Ducketts, were confiscated by the Crown as part of the Dissolution of the Monasteries, masterminded by Thomas Cromwell, who ten years earlier had been Chief Steward of Tottenham.

The estate was sold by the Crown in 1547, along with other properties, for £1,160. 10s. 3d. to Richard Cecil, Henry's Yeoman of the Wardrobe, and in turn to Sir Edward North, then Court Chancellor. Later as Lord North he was involved in the conspiracy to secure the nine-day reign of Lady Jane Grey on the English throne following the death of Edward VI in 1553. In 1580 the estate passed to John Dudley, who was also lord of the manor of Stoke Newington, and who was closely involved in the Elizabethan court. By 1619 the estate had passed to Sir Francis Popham, the soldier and politician, who had married John Dudley's daughter.

BOUNDS AND WOODLEIGH

This estate, recorded in 1342, in the north-west of the area also included land in Edmonton, but its precise boundaries are not clear. It was held by a succession of private individuals until it came into the hands of Edward III in c. 1375, who granted it to the Charterhouse monastery in 1378.

In 1463 the estate comprised 146 acres of which Bounds Wood and Austynsredding were located to the north of Tottenham Wood on the west of Bounds Green Road. Following the Dissolution of the Monasteries (in 1538) Bounds Wood of 60 acres passed to Lord (Edward) North and in 1565 to Sir Thomas Wroth (1518-73). Wroth was also involved in the plot to install Jane Seymour on the English throne. Bounds Wood eventually became part of the Bowes Manor Estate.

DEARS PIGHTLE AND BAKERSFIELD

These two small entities totalling 6 acres were to the north of Wood Green Common and in 1455 were held by the Prioress of Kilburn. Between 1335-6 they were leased to John Wheeler and seized by the Crown at the Dissolution and sold to Henry Audley and John Cordell in 1544. Today, Dears Pightle is delineated by St Michaels Terrace, Dorset Road and Terrick Road. Bakersfield became part of the Nightingale Hall Estate and is now occupied by Nightingale Gardens and the west side of Park Avenue.

WOODREDDINGS

Woodreddings was a copyhold estate cleared from the eastern flank of Tottenham Wood, of about 60 acres on the south of Bounds Green Road; it was recorded as 'le Woderedynge' in a grant dated 1392. Amongst its tenants were John de Northampton, a draper and once Sheriff (1376) and Lord Mayor (1382) of London and lord of the manor of Daubeneys (1391); William and Robert Ederiche (in the late 15th century) both prominent Wood Green residents; Sir John Skevington, another Sheriff of London (1520); and William Locke, citizen and mercer of London, in 1545. Woodreddings passed to Elizabeth Locke, grand-daughter of William Locke, in 1566 who by the early Elizabethan period had become the wife of Richard Candeler, a Middlesex JP, the first Tottenham resident to own the estate. One of Candeler's interesting cases as a magistrate involved Agnes Godfrey accused in 1597, 1610 and 1613 of being the 'Witch Of Enfield'. But unlike others similarly accused at that time she was acquitted on each charge.

AUSTYNSREDDING

Austynsredding was a 14-acre freehold plot to the north of Woodreddings, and was the subject of a grant to a Gilbert de Fox in 1356. It was still woodland in 1599 when surveyed by Israel Amyce who was commissioned by the Dean and Chapter of St Paul's to survey all woods adjacent to their properties in Tottenham and Edmonton. At that time reference was made to undergrowth four years old, evidence perhaps of coppicing. Austynsredding was combined with Woodreddings to form the Nightingale Hall estate in the 18th century and today it forms the western part of the Albert Road Recreation Ground.

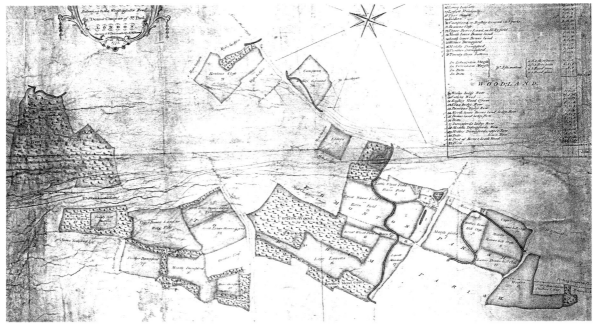

5. *Extract from a map showing the manor of Bowes Farm, dated 1778.*

BOWES FARM MANOR ESTATE

A large part of the north-western reaches of Wood Green once formed part of the manors of Bowes and Dernford, which date from Norman times. In 1412 King Henry IV granted these to the Dean and Chapter of St Paul's Cathedral. One of the sub-manors was Bowes and Polehouse and this was sub-let as two farms based on Bowes and Polehouse respectively, each of which was leased separately from the 16th century.

The Bowes Farm estate contained about 370 acres, of which 200 or so lay in the Wood Green ward of the parish of Tottenham. It included large tracts of woodland, which survived to the end of the 18th century, to the west of Bounds Green Road. More woodland extended from Bounds Green Road to the High Road. The estate also included land to the east of the High Road and east of Wolves Lane (now part of the New River Sports Ground).

During the 17th century some parts of the estate in Wood Green became freehold but the major part remained in the hands of the Dean and Chapter of St Paul's, and later the Ecclesiastical Commissioners, leased as Wood Green Farm and as part of Bounds Green Farm. In 1804 the estate was leased in six lots to private individuals and subsequently sold. Some of these lots in Wood Green were to become sites for housing developments in the latter half of the 19th century.

The moated Bowes Farm manor house, dating from the 14th century, was located in Palmers Green just north of the Tottenham parish boundary to the west of the High Road where are now Sidney and Melbourne Avenues. In the 19th century Bowes Manor, as the house was known – and by this time a splendid property surrounded by landscaped gardens – was the residence of Thomas Wilde, who later became Lord Truro. He was followed by Thomas Sidney, an alderman of the City of London and Lord Mayor (1853-54), who resided there until his death in 1889.

HOPPERSFIELD

This 8-acre copyhold estate was at the corner of what is now the High Road and White Hart Lane. In 1533 it passed into the Ederiche family who were prominent Wood Green residents and in 1619 a substantial house stood there. In the mid-19th century the property was owned by George Francis King, a City tavern keeper. The site was later occupied by the Kings Arms public house.

CAPPERS

Cappers, comprising 70 acres, was to the south of Wood Green Common with Tottenham Wood to the west, the parish of Hornsey to the south and Mayes Road on the east. It was held by a Robert Warner in 1531-43 and subsequently passed to the Wheeler family who were influential local residents during the 17th century.

THE TUDOR PERIOD

By the time of the long reign of Henry VIII (1509-47), the hamlet of Wood Green features in the proceedings of the Tottenham manor court. A Constable for the ward was appointed annually from that date. The Edrich family appear in the records:' John Edrich of Woodgreene' in 1531, and 'Thomas Ederyche of Woodgreen' in 1545. The rolls reveal much evidence of illegal tree felling and enclosure of common land, as well as the failure of landowners to scour ditches and maintain bridges over streams.

THE DORSET SURVEY, 1619

Thomas, Earl of Dorset, became lord of the manor of Tottenham in 1605. He instituted a major survey of his domains in 1619 which provided a detailed picture of land ownership and usage. The first reliable plan of the parish of Tottenham, by I.T Barrow, accompanied the survey.

At this time the Wood Green ward covered the western half of the parish of Tottenham, bounded on the south-east by Stoke Newington, on the west by Hornsey and to the north by Edmonton. Its south-eastern reaches included the hamlet of West Green, Hangers Green, Chisley (later Hanger) Lane, Blackhope Lane (now part of West Green Road) and part of Philip Lane. The southernmost part, on the east side of Green Lanes was ecclesiastical land belonging to the Priory of St John of Jerusalem in Clerkenwell. Its northern parts, including Bounds Green and the land surrounding Chitts Hill, which was high ground at the junction of today's Woodside and Cross Roads, and left blank on the plan, were part of the Bowes Manor estate then in the hands of the Dean and Chapter of St Paul's Cathedral.

Wood Green was thinly populated with about 50 people occupying sixteen houses. Nine of the larger of these houses border the Wood Green itself, the others being at the corner of the High Road and White Hart Lane (the location of Hoppersfield). Four of the larger houses on the north side of the common backed on to the New River and may have been only recently built,

taking advantage of the new amenity. There were eight houses around West Green. A number of cottages, not depicted in the plan, are also mentioned in the text of the survey.

The commons included Beans Green, Hangers Green, Ducketts Green and West Green to the south, and in the north, in addition to Wood Green and Chapmans Green (at the junction of Lordship Lane and Perth Road), there were Elses Green (the crossroads at High Road and Lordship Lane) and Smyths Cross Green (junction of High Road and Bounds Green Road).

Most woodland in the eastern half of the Tottenham parish had been cleared but a significant amount remained in the Wood Green area. Tottenham Wood itself had been reduced but according to the Survey it:

> contayneth 388 acres 2 roods. there are within the same about 4660 Tymber Trees worth to be presently sold according to the rate of 3s. 4d the Tree – £776. 13s. 4d. The underwood is of divers growth and is presently mostly at 30s the acre one with another – £583. 2s. 6d.

Hawke Parke adjacent to Ducketts comprised 74 acres and contained 388 trees and underwood of 7 to 9 years old as a result of coppicing. Much of the other woodland had been cleared, except for a few groves to the east of Chapmans Green, making way for pasture and arable fields. About half of the Ducketts estate was still shown as groves.

As well as the New River through the northern part of Wood Green, the plan shows the Moselle and the Stonebridge stream running from the west across the area towards the river Lea. A loop in the Moselle on the south side of Lordship Lane enclosed several fields known as Broadwaters, later to become Broadwater Farm.

One of the principal landowners in the area at this time was Mrs Elizabeth Candeler, widow of Richard Candeler JP who held Woodreddings (see above). The Candelers lived at Tottenham Green and are commemorated in the church of All Hallows, Tottenham, in a fine veiled marble vault adorned with kneeling figures.

The Wheeler family were also prominent in the Survey. They owned most of the land surrounding the common and 141 acres of freehold property including Cappers, Mayes and other parcels. Thomas Wheeler had his house and orchard on the south side of the green. He became lord of the manor briefly in 1600 by virtue of redeeming a mortgage on the manor forfeited by Sir William

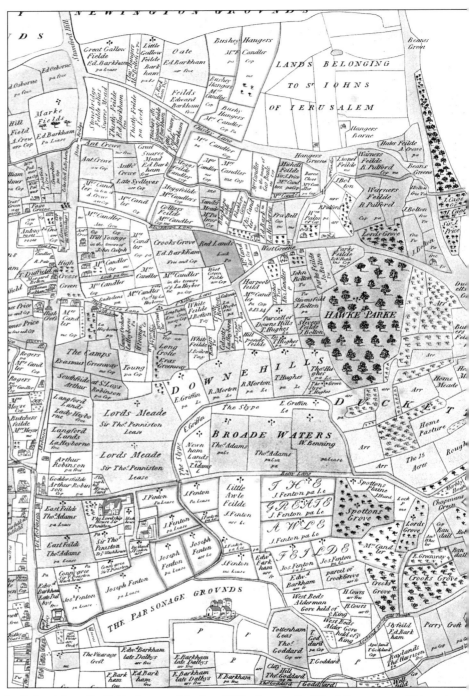

6. Extract from the Tottenham parish plan, 1619, showing the Wood Green area. This first detailed map of the parish accompanied a survey authorised by the Earl of Dorset, then lord of the manor. North is to the foot of the map.

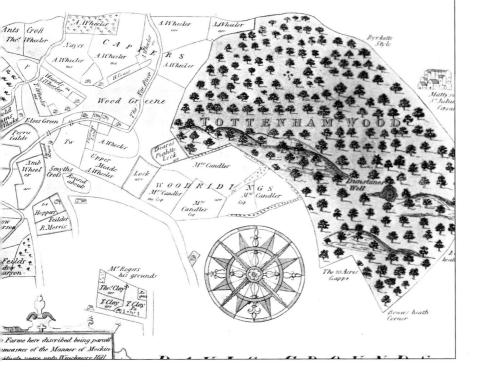

HARNSEY GROVNDS

7. *Monument commemorating Richard and Elizabeth Candeler in All Hallows Church, Tottenham.*

Compton. He was described by William Bedwell (1631) as a *'procteur of Arches'* (ecclesiastical advocate) and a wealthy man. In his will of 1611 he left 'twelve pence per week for ever, to be given in bread unto the poorest sort, especially those of Wood-greene.' He was also a dissenter and fined accordingly for 'not attending church or chapel or usual place of Common Prayer.'

At this time Ducketts Manor and Farm was held by Sir Francis Popham (see above), who sold it in 1639 for £2800 to Sir Edmund Scott of Lambeth in whose family it remained until 1660.

TOTTENHAM WOOD

Tottenham Wood, or *Tottenham Hanger* (a wooded hill), was once a prominent landmark on the western flank of the parish of Tottenham occupying a substantial part of the Wood Green Ward.

In the 12th century William Fitzstephen, chaplain to King Henry II, in his *Description of the City of London*, described the suburbs to the north of London:

> Beyond them an immense forest extends itself beautified with woods and groves full of the lairs and coverts of beasts and game, stags, bucks, wild boars and wild bulls.

Deforestation in Middlesex began from about 1218 but Tottenham Wood in common with Enfield Chase survived for several centuries, both becoming a last refuge for wild animals. It was these that attracted the interest of King James I, who, in the early 17th century, enclosed the woodland for his exclusive use for hunting. In 1623 his secretary wrote to those responsible for the Wood thus:

> The King is much incovenienced in his hunting in Tottenham Woods by the want of convenient gates, and they damaged by the fences being ridden over and broken down. His Majesty wishes them to cause gates to be made for the convenient passage, and if they are to be kept locked, one key to be sent to him which will be reserved for his exclusive use.

The eventual clearance of Tottenham Wood began by Act of Parliament in 1777 after which it became Tottenham Wood Farm.

The Wood also became part of local folklore with two proverbs first recorded by Bedwell but in fact of much earlier origin. One, relating to things not achievable and alluding to the size of the hill and wood:

> You shall as easily remove Tottenham Wood

The other:

> When Tottenham Wood is all on fire
> Then Tottenham Street is nought but mire

The interpretation of which was that when the wood was enveloped in mist, giving an impression of smoke, the resulting wet weather would have obvious consequences in Tottenham street or village.

These proverbs led to Tottenham Wood being immortalised in verse in 1820 by John Abraham Heraud Jnr. (1799-1887). His long, and probably his first, poem *The Hermitage, or the Legend of St Loy*, related to Tottenham Wood. As a whole it received commendation from the then Poet Laureate, Robert Southey, but local historian, Dr William Robinson, was less happy and encouraged Heraud to rewrite it to be 'more general in its description of Tottenham and its antiquities.' As a result Heraud wrote another poem called *Tottenham* in 1821, which also contained two verses relating to the wood. Heraud went on to become a distinguished poet and was drama critic of the *Illustrated London News* from 1849-79.

Tottenham Wood was also celebrated for the curative properties of St Dunstan's Well situated within it. After the wood was cleared the well remained in a meadow named after it until the latter part of the 19th century – its site is now the junction of Albert and Victoria Roads.

Tottenham Wood was also the refuge of two Catholic priests, John Brushford and John Todd, who attempted to re-establish their faith in England after the Reformation. They are said to have stayed in a cottage in the wood to avoid detection by the authorities.

8. The New River by Myddleton Road. Watercolour by C. Yardley c.1870.

A New River

By the beginning of the 17th century the City of London was in dire need of a better fresh water supply for its increasing population. In 1603 some 30,000 Londoners had died of a 'plague', i.e. an epidemic attributed to a lack of sanitation.

The idea of a man-made river, first proposed by Edmund Colthurst in 1600, to bring water from the natural springs at Chadwell and Amwell in Hertfordshire to the heights of Clerkenwell in London was enshrined in an Acts of Parliament of 1606 and 1607. The project, a major civil engineering feat of its time, was assigned to Sir Hugh Myddelton and his New River Company. He received substantial personal and financial support from King James I and construction was carried out between 1609 and 1613.

The ten-foot wide and four-foot deep river followed closely the 100-foot (33m) contour along its course with a very shallow gradient to provide a steady flow. As a consequence the river took a meandering 38-mile course on its way south, particularly through Wood Green, which was reached in July 1612. It entered the area on the west of the High Road, flowing south to opposite today's Woodside Park where it crossed the High Road and turned abruptly north and then east to skirt around what was then called Chitts Hill, running back into the parish of Edmonton and then returning to Wood Green, around Devonshire Hill. It then went south-west to cross the High Road again just north of Wood Green Underground station, and along the north side of Wood Green Common, turning south across the middle of the common into Hornsey.

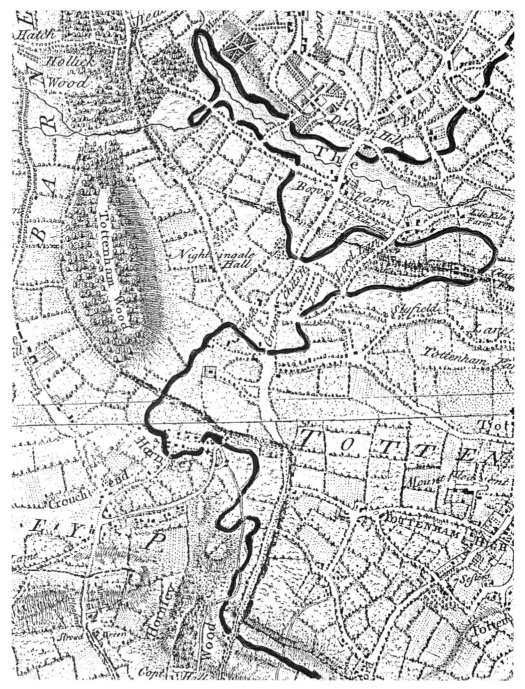

9. *John Rocque's map of Middlesex, 1754, showing the original meandering course of the New River through the Wood Green area.*

10. *The New River Tunnel, southern entrance, viewed from Station Road c. 1903.*

11. *A view of White Hart Lane c.1880, looking west to St Michael's Church, with the New River in the foreground*

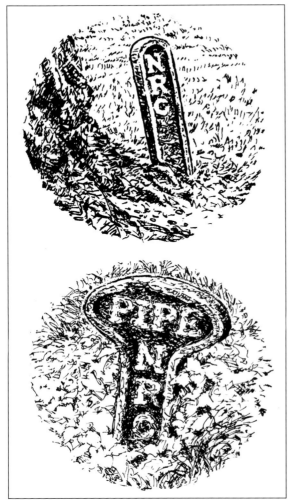

12. New River Company boundary and tunnel markers, still in Avenue Gardens. Drawings by Peter Garland.

The building of the river brought several hundred labourers into an otherwise tranquil rural area, albeit temporarily. Its construction met with financial and practical problems, including opposition from local landowners, but was completed on 29 September 1613 when its waters flowed into the New River Head near Sadler's Wells, Clerkenwell. In the course of building the river, the New River Company acquired a substantial amount of land in the Wood Green area, which was subsequently leased or rented to local landowners. This and the course of the river led to the first significant changes of the estate pattern in the locality and the destruction of many trees, much lamented by local historian William Bedwell.

Up to the mid-19th century the watercourse enhanced the reputation of Wood Green by providing an attractive location for the larger houses of the more wealthy citizens, such as those along the north side of Wood Green Common (by 1619), Harringay House (*c.*1792), Wood Green House (*c.*1780) and Chitts Hill House (*c.*1805)

But by 1850 there was a need to increase the flow of the water and the meandering loop of the river around Chitts Hill and Devonshire Hill was shortened by means of a 1100-yard long, fourteen-feet diameter tunnel, built between 1852-59, from Myddleton Road to Station Road (the tunnel entrances are now Grade II listed). As a consequence the redundant section of the river to the east of the High Road gradually dried up and the land became available for other uses. The section between Devonshire Hill and Wolves Lane eventually became the New River Playing Fields.

The original course of the river through Wood Green and Tottenham is reflected in a number of later street names, such as River Park Road and Rivulet Road, and the subsequent layout of certain roads, such as Pellatt Grove, was determined by the old course of the river.

The building of the tunnel allowed the creation of a 'green route' through the northern part of Wood Green. The land above the tunnel was leased to the local authority and by the beginning of the 20th century had become the public open spaces known as Finsbury Gardens, Nightingale Gardens, and part of Avenue Gardens. Some of the original iron markers defining the New River Company's boundaries and the line of the tunnel can be seen in these gardens.

After a period of uncertainty about its future in the 1980s, the New River between Enfield and Stoke Newington was given a new lease of life by its current owners, Thames Water. This involved the sinking of bore-holes along its route to take advantage of the natural aquifers for water storage. Two of the associated neatly designed pump-houses, built in the early 1990s, can be seen at either end of the Wood Green tunnel.

Highways and Local Ways

THE HIGH ROAD

The high road through Wood Green forms part of the 'Green Lanes', a route which runs from Shoreditch just north of the City via the present Southgate Road in Hackney to Newington Green, along the west side of Clissold Park to the Manor House. From here it entered the parish of Tottenham passing through Harringay, by Ducketts Green and Wood Green and on to Palmers Green, Enfield, Hertford and the north. The origin of this road is obscure.

As has already been noted (p.8), the Romans made two major military supply roads through the Middlesex forest. One of them, Ermine Street, ran due north from Bishopsgate via Stamford Hill to west of the river Lea to Waltham Abbey and on to Lincoln and York. Earlier historians suggested the 'green lanes' in the west of the parish formed part of Ermine Street, a view supported by both Bedwell and local historian Richard Dyson. Bedwell (1631) records:

> in King John's time about the year of our Lord 1210, the great rode [road] out of the North lay through Hartford, and from thence to Hatfield, and so through the Chace [Enfield Chase] to Southgate, Boes [Bowes Manor], Wood-greene, Dou'cotes [Ducketts] along to Stone Bridge, neere the confines of Tottenham, Hornsey, and Newington, and so through Islington to London.

However, it has later been accepted that Ermine Street became the Tottenham High Road (today the A10 and A1010), a typically straight road to the east although it has been suggested that the 'green lanes' also existed then and was used when Ermine Street was flooded by the Lea. Fisk (1913) describes the high road as 'an ancient Basilical way', but without substantiation. However, most historians agree that the high road was of some antiquity and Roe (1949) contends that Ermine Street dates only from AD250, with the implication that the high road would have been in use before that.

In early times the road connected a series of greens which were recorded in the 14th century. The first on entering the parish at Manor House was Beans Green, between the present Endymion

Road and St Ann's Road, forming the Harringay section of Green Lanes. To the north it passed Ducketts Green on its west and then Ducketts Manor and Farm to the east before crossing the Moselle beyond which lay Elses Green, now the junction of High Road and Lordship Lane. The road then rose steeply up to Smyths Cross Green at the junction with Bounds Green Road. This section of the high road later became known as Jolly Butchers Hill (*see* p90). It then continued north to Palmers Green.

The high road was used by drovers, avoiding the busier road through Tottenham village, to take livestock to the London cattle market at Smithfield and the fairs at Bow and Stepney.

The increased use of roads during the 18th century called for better maintenance. This was delegated by Parliament to Turnpike Trusts who installed tollgates and levied tolls on travellers. In return the Trusts laid improved roads using the techniques of Macadam and carried out repairs. The high road through Wood Green was found to be a convenient route of avoiding payment of tolls at the Whetstone tollgate on the Great North Road through Highgate and this led to an Act for the establishment of the Hornsey Toll Gate of 1710 which states:

> And whereas there is a passage (lying in the said Parish of Tottenham and Edmonton or one of them) called Wood Green through which Stage Coaches, Calashes, Carts, Waggons, Drovers, Packhorses, Higlers and divers other persons travelling to London, since the erecting of the Turnpike at Whetsone [on the Great North Road] in the Parish of Fryan Barnet in the summer season, have come and passed, by which they have evaded payment to the said Turnpike and if the same shall continue, by reason of some passages that also lead thereunto out of the High Road from the said Parish of Enfield to London, the Turnpikes or Turnpikes to be set up by this Act in the High Road aforesaid, will not be of the use intended or raise money designed by the said Act ...

Thereby, the Hornsey Toll House at the corner of the eastern end of Tottenham Lane (later Turnpike Lane) was established and tolls levied from 1739 but the gate itself was not operational until 1765 under the authority of the Stamford Hill and Green Lanes Turnpike Trust. The Hornsey Toll Gate was the only gate across Green Lanes until 1792.

The gate and its keepers, in common with

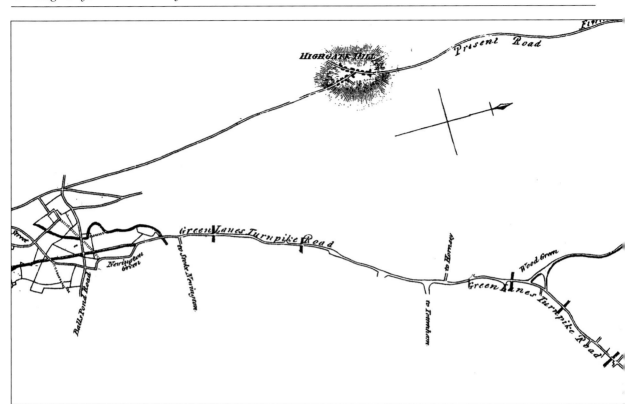

13. *Plan of the proposed 'New North Road', 1810. It shows the Green Lanes turnpike road and a new branch from Wood Green to Whetstone.*

others, were much resented and the subject of many incidents during its existence. The notorious highwayman, Dick Turpin (1709-39), is reported in contemporary accounts to have once made a visit to Wood Green when his famous steed Black Bess carried him over the high Hornsey Toll Gate, surmounted with spikes, when being pursued by a posse led by the chief constable of Westminster.

In 1826 authority for the turnpikes passed to the Metropolis Roads Commissioners. The turnpike system was abandoned in 1872 and the Hornsey Toll Gate demolished. Responsibility for road maintenance then passed to the Tottenham Local Board of Health and to the Wood Green Local Board of Health on its creation in 1888. By this time parts of Green Lanes had been renamed. Between Turnpike Lane and the top of Jolly Butchers Hill, just north of today's Wood Green Underground station, was still known as Green Lanes; but from the Hill to Canning Crescent became the High Street, and from there to the Palmers Green border became

Southgate Road. Soon after the creation of the Urban District Council in 1894 the whole length of the road from Turnpike Lane to Lascotts Road became the Wood Green High Road, which it remains today.

14. *Hornsey Turnpike Gatehouse after closure in 1872.*

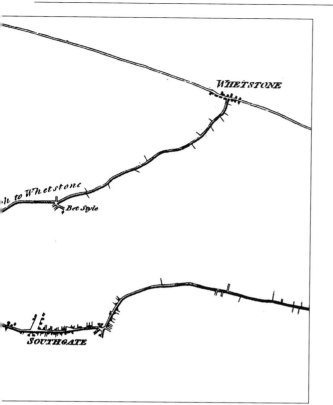

BYWAYS

The principal tributary of the high road was Bounds Lane (later Bounds Green Road). This ran from the 6-mile stone on the high road, to Bounds Green and on to Whetstone. Established by the 14th century, it was a wide track with all the characteristics of a drove road and its grass verges are still very much in evidence today. A Vestry minute of 1794 records that arising from complaints about its 'ruinous and dangerous condition' it should be 'mended as a Drift [or Drove] Way'; this avoided any serious expenditure by the Vestry. A plan of 1810 shows that Bounds Lane had become a branch, from Wood Green to Whetstone, of 'The New North Road' from London to Potters Bar (which followed Green Lanes). This upgrading of Bounds Lane superseded a proposal in 1809 to forge a new road from Wood Green to Whetstone via Colney Hatch across Wood Green Common. The wide verges, particularly on the west side of Bounds Green Road remained largely undeveloped until the turn of the 20th century when some were laid out as public gardens.

15. Allegedly, a picture of Dick Turpin 'Clearing the old Hornsey toll bar gate to the surprise of his pursuers'. A contemporary print.

16. A watercolour view of Green Lanes, 1850.

The 1619 Dorset Survey map (*see* p14) shows several lanes between Green Lanes and Tottenham Street, or the Tottenham High Road as it became known. These were of much earlier origin connecting the various clearings in the medieval forest; they are mentioned without names in the early manorial court records and are considered to pre-date a survey of 1429. Lordship Lane (known as Berry Lane in 1619) ran easterly as it does today from the high road to Tottenham High Road via Chapmans Green and Bruce Castle. Its present name derives from the Lordship House, as Bruce Castle was once known. Two other links between Green Lanes and Tottenham High Road lay to the south. Chisley Lane (now St Ann's Road) connected Beans Green and Hangers Green with Tottenham High Road to the south of the Stonebridge stream. Another lane, now West Green Road, connected Ducketts Green with West Green and then diverged via West Green Road to Tottenham High Cross.

The meandering Apeland Street of 1619, known as Styfield Lane in the 18th century and later as White Hart Lane, led from Smyths Cross Green, at the junction of the high road and Bounds Green Road, via Searles Green to the northern end of Tottenham High Road. In Tudor times a broad green lane, 'Shutteslane', led north from White Hart Lane to Chitts Hill, an area of common at the junction of Woodside Road and Cross

Road; this is no longer a thoroughfare and is occupied by Riversdale Gardens and the southern part of Glendale Avenue. Blind Lane and Snakes Lane, connected Chapmans Green with White Hart Lane: Blind Lane survived as an alley at the rear of houses in Acacia and Dunbar Roads until the redevelopment of the area in the 1960s. Wolf (now Wolves) Lane led north from White Hart Lane to connect with Tilekiln Lane (now Tottenhall Road) in Palmers Green. The name derives from Woolls, once a parcel of woodland on the east side of the lane, part of the Bowes Manor estate and now forming part of the New River Playing Fields. Devonshire Hill Lane led from White Hart Lane to Clay Hill. Mayes or Maizes Lane (Mayes Road) ran the short distance from the west of Green Lanes, opposite Ducketts manor house, bridging the Moselle stream, to the Wood Green itself.

Tottenham Lane, which led from Green Lanes at Ducketts Green to Hornsey village was, as its name implies, the main route between Hornsey and Tottenham villages. Following the creation of the Hornsey turnpike the eastern end became known as Turnpike Lane.

The upkeep of the local roads and lanes was once under the jurisdiction of the parish vestry and was carried out by local people. The vestry minutes record that at the beginning of the 18th century Wood Green people, like many elsewhere, were reluctant to carry out their statutory

17. White Hart Lane 1880. A rustic view by William Oliphant.

18. Lordship Lane, 1893.

work, thereby incurring fines.

This pattern of roads and lanes remained unchanged from medieval times until the latter half of the 19th century when the building of residential streets began. Nevertheless, some of the lanes, particularly Devonshire Hill Lane, White Hart Lane and Wolves Lane retained their rural charm, with tall hedgerows and overhanging trees, well into the 20th century. They are important thoroughfares today. Snakes Lane also survived into the 20th century but became Perth Road by the 1920s.

19. Snakes Lane 1902. It was renamed Perth Road in the 1920s. Photograph by J.G.S. Mummery.

Farms from Forest

Farming in the parish of Tottenham began in the 13th century following the deforestation of parts of the Middlesex forest, but Tottenham Wood and a large amount of coppiced woodland still existed in the Wood Green area at the beginning of the 17th century. By1800 most of the woodland had been cleared to be replaced by pasture and arable fields and Wood Green had become very much a farming community. This is portrayed in Thomas Milne's survey of land usage in Middlesex published in 1800 and supported in a local Tottenham survey conducted by local landowner Edward Wyburd in 1798. Both surveys were accompanied by plans detailing actual usage of fields i.e. arable, meadow, orchard etc. and they are particularly informative. Arable land was used mainly for wheat and hay with some oats. The meadows and pasture were for grazing, mainly dairy and beef cattle and sheep. Farms had their own kitchen gardens and orchards. The 1831 census showed that in Wood

Green ward there were 55 persons engaged in agriculture plus 65 agricultural labourers. The 1843 Tottenham Rent Charge Returns also allow the ownership, tenancy and size of Wood Green's farms to be determined

Each of the early estates became a farm in its own right with ownership remaining in the hands of the landed gentry, while the land was worked by tenant farmers. The size of the farms varied from a few tens of acres to a few hundreds.

FROM DUCKETTS TO DOVECOTE

By the mid-17th century the ownership of Ducketts Farm had passed to Edmund Trench, described as 'doctor of Physick' and remained in the Trench family for several generations. In 1741 it passed by marriage to John Berney, but by 1776 a part of Ducketts, which became Grainger's farm, passed to Richard Muilman Trench Chiswell, a London merchant and antiquary.

For most of the 17th century Ducketts was farmed by the Benning family. Francis Benning was Upper Churchwarden of All Hallows,

20. *Extract from Milne's Land Use map of Middlesex, 1800. The map describes the usage of fields: arable (a), meadow (m), woodland (w) and private parklands (p).*

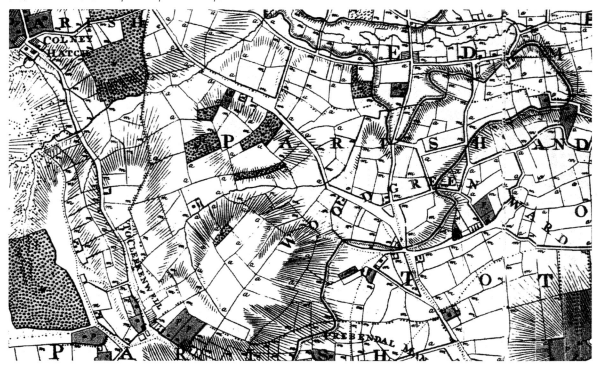

21. Duckett's farmhouse on the east side of the High Road, a 'compact residence ... surrounded by a moat'. From Robinson's History and Antiquities of Tottenham, 1840.

Tottenham, 1638-39 and his son, William, was elected Constable of Hornsey in 1624. Thomas and Matthew Benning enlisted in 1626 as members of the Trained Band Militia, a sort of volunteer army which was trained to deal with civil unrest, but evidence of their active involvement is not known. In 1644, during the Civil War, Thomas Benning was Collector of Weekly Assessments, a tax levied to support the Parliamentary cause. In 1664 he was elected Heyward of the Marshes and in the same year John Benning was elected Marker of Cattle.

The tenure of Ducketts Farm by the Benning family ended in 1707 and the tenancy for the next seventy years still needs to be established. From 1776 until 1801 it was held by John Wilmot who, in 1795, successfully applied to the manorial court to erect a pound close to Ducketts to hold all stray cattle encroaching the commons and waste lands in the Wood Green ward of the parish; this was to supplement the other parish pound situated in Tottenham village. James Angle

tenanted the farm from 1801 to 1821. At the end of Angle's tenancy Ducketts Farm was put up for sale. It included

> a compact residence, offices, garden, orchard, yards and out-buildings surrounded by a moat, and an enclosed farm yard, with barns, stables etc. and sundry enclosures of meadow and arable land containing 140 acres, 2 roods and 5 perches(including 115 acres meadow and 14 acres arable) , bounded by a stream of water and the turnpike road from Tottenham to Southgate, Hornsey etc ...

The asking price was £15,000 but the sale did not take place and Ducketts Farm remained in the Berney family until 1840 when it was purchased by Alfred Jones, a banker, who remained in possession until 1879. In 1841 the farm was leased to William Duckworth, a cattle agent, who farmed there for six years after which a Mr Tatler took possession and was the last tenant farmer at Ducketts. By this time the holding specialised in the raising of beef cattle. An auction of the contents of the farm held on 2 September 1862 listed:

> 20 Handsome short-horn heifers (many in calf),
> 2 Bulls.
> A well-bred English Horse 'Young Day Break' and a thoroughbred
> ditto by 'Amorena'
> 2 mares in foal, and 2 ditto with foals
> 1 Five year old filly
> 4 Promising Yearling Colts
> 1 Nag Mare and pony
> 2 6-inch wheel Hay Carts
> 1 Spring Van and other implements
> 4 Stacks and a stump of prime Meadow hay containing about 200 loads.

Thomas Clark, a professional soldier turned property developer, took a lease from Jones on Ducketts manor and Farm in 1862 to build twelve pairs of houses and villas along the Green Lanes frontage. The arrival of the Great Eastern Railway in 1878 was to seal the fate of Ducketts, by then known as Dovecote Farm, which it traversed. The farm was sold for development within a few years to make way for the Noel Park Estate.

GRAINGER'S FARM

Grainger's Farm formed the eastern half of Ducketts, bordered by the Moselle. In the mid-18th century it was tenanted by Thomas Phillips, a Quaker, who farmed elsewhere in Tottenham. Following the death of Richard Trench Chiswell (see above) in 1798 the farm, comprising 69 acres was purchased by Michael and John Phillips for £3,890; they were also tenants at the nearby Broadwater Farm for 70 years until 1861. The elder brother, Michael, effectively managed both Grainger's and Broadwater Farms.

The farm remained in the Phillips family until 1844 when it contained 70 acres with Henry Carr as tenant. It was purchased in 1880 by the British Land Company for development but it survived almost to the end of the 19th century before it too succumbed to the inevitable urbanisation.

TENT FARM

Tent Farm is shown on the 1864 O.S. Map on the north-side of White Hart Lane close to the Tottenham boundary. In 1843 the fields adjacent to the farmhouse were owned by William Dover and occupied by Johnathan Thomas. This land became the location of Cole's and South's Potteries by the 1860s.

22. Tottenham Wood Farmhouse in c.1930, then used by Muswell Hill Golf Club. From the Wood Green Guide.

TOTTENHAM WOOD FARM

The deforestation of Tottenham Wood did not begin until 1777 and the estate was put up for auction in 1789. Robinson (1840) describes it at the time of auction as:

> A freehold estate consisting of Tottenham Wood, near to Muswell Hill (most of which was then cleared and cultivated) also of several meadow lands adjoining containing in the whole 367 acres and 33 perches, more or less, part of which was in hand and the remainder let to tenants.

A farmhouse and other buildings existed at this time but were located within the manor of Hornsey.

The estate was purchased by Michael Mitchell, a City tobacconist, for £11,410. He built a new farmhouse alongside today's Rhodes Avenue, and effected many improvements. On his death the farm was bought by Thomas Rhodes (1763-1856). The Rhodes family (of whom the colonialist, Cecil Rhodes was a later member) were established farmers in Staffordshire from the early part of the 17th century. In the 18th century William Rhodes came south, establishing farms in St Pancras, Islington and Leyton. His descendant Thomas Rhodes built up a substantial dairy farm, the largest in the parish of Tottenham, but never quite reached his aim of 1,000 cows. By 1843 the farm occupied 379 acres and only 30 perches of the original Tottenham Wood remained.

In 1850 the farm was increased with the aquisition of part of the neighbouring Nightingale Hall Farm on its eastern flank. Thomas Rhodes died in 1856 aged 93 outliving both his wife and son, also named Thomas; all three were interred in All Hallows churchyard, Tottenham. By 1861 the farm was in the hands of Margaret Rhodes, widow of Thomas Rhodes jnr. and comprised 424 acres in total. It was sold shortly after on the direction of the will of Thomas Rhodes snr. for the benefit of his grandchildren. The major part of the farmland was to have a new lease of life as Alexandra Park and another part became Muswell Hill Golf Course, for which the farmhouse became the club house until 1932 when it was demolished except for the portico which today stands surrounded by trees at the corner of Rhodes Avenue.

NIGHTINGALE HALL FARM

Farming activity on the Woodreddings estate, cut out of the eastern flank of Tottenham Wood, was documented in the 14th century when it contained 25 acres. By 1619 it had expanded to several fields totalling 60 acres, tenanted by a Robert Morris and in 1732 it had grown to 72 acres 'with barns, stables and outbuildings'. In 1769 it was combined with the adjacent Austynsredding and became known as Nightingale Hall Farm. In 1798 its copyhold tenant was John Giles and was sub-let to Thomas Dale, the son of a stable-keeper in the City. The Poor Rate books of that time show Dale as farming elsewhere in Tottenham. During the first half of the 19th century the copyhold passed to the Woodward family and in 1843 Mary Ann Woodward extended the estate to include Dears Pightle and Bakersfield, on its southern boundary, increasing its size to 88 acres. From about 1820 much of the pasture was tenanted by Thomas Rhodes. The coming of the Great Northern Railway in 1850 split the farm in two, and the major slice to the west became part of Tottenham Wood Farm, while the fields to the east remained attached to Nightingale Hall.

WOOD GREEN FARM

Wood Green Farm occupied the triangle of land formed by Bounds Green Road and the High Road, north of today's St Michael's Church, with its northern boundary defined by today's Clarence and Truro Roads. It had once been part of the Bowes Manor Farm estate but had become freehold by the late 17th century.

In 1798 this farm was owned by William Wrangham, who lived in Palmers Green. At that time it totalled 57 acres of arable and pasture farmed by Thomas King, who also rented 55 acres of land to the east of the High Road being part of the Chitts Hill estate, and a further 20 acres at Bounds Green. King, who lived in Edmonton, also farmed extensively in that parish. By 1843 the Wood Green Farm and other fields at Bounds Green, totalling 99 acres, were owned by James Foster and occupied by Frederick Attenbring who also tenanted fields at Bounds Green. In the mid-19th century Wood Green Farm was also known as 'The Grass Farm' suggesting its main produce. In 1853 Wood Green Farm was the first farm in the area to be sold *in toto* for large-scale house building.

23. Devonshire Hill Farm House, rear view, c.1910.

CLAY HILL FARM

This farm lay to the south of Clay Hill, later known as Devonshire Hill, at the north-eastern extremity of Wood Green ward between White Hart Lane and the parish boundary with Edmonton. It stood in the loop of the New River which flowed around the east side of Clay Hill. Much of the land either side of the river, and the farmstead, was acquired by the New River Company which leased it to the local farmers.

By 1798 the farm 90 acres owned by the Duke of Northumberland and then farmed by Thomas Duck. In 1843 it was occupied by Thomas Wilson Robinson with 82 acres to the south of White Hart Lane and 57 acres on the west of Wolves Lane leased from the New River Company. Thomas Robinson was a silk merchant who lived in the farmhouse at Devonshire Hill. In the 1860s the 145-acre farm was occupied by Henry Thompson and known as Thompson's Farm. Census returns for 1871 and 1881 show that 4-5 men were employed on the farm.

By 1890 the farm was called Devonshire Hill Farm. It has been suggested this name derives from the fact that the Augustinian Canons upon whom King David I of Scotland had bestowed Tottenham Church also held land at Clayhanger, near Crediton, in Devon.

Between 1890 and the early 1920s the farmhouse was occupied by Samuel South (of South's Potteries) and his family. The Souths also rented part of the farm for pasture and growing hay for their cart-horses which were stabled there. The farmhouse survived until the 1920s and one of the cottages was still occupied in 1941. The farmland on the north side of White Hart Lane became the New River Playing Fields and later the New River Sports Centre.

24. A rural scene at Bounds Green c.1800. Watercolour by William Payne.

25. Bounds Green Farmhouse in 1924.

BOUNDS GREEN FARM

Bounds Green Farm covered the north-western reaches of the Wood Green area to the west of Bounds Green Road and extended north from the Muswell Stream (along the line of today's Albert Road) to Bounds Green Brook (today the line of the Pinkham Road section of the North Circular Road), covering an area of 200 acres or so. About half of it was part of the Bowes Manor Farm estate and in 1778 it still included 80 acres of woodland and substantial hedgerows. At this time the farm was in the ownership of John Beardmore and farmed by Charles Hutchins.

In 1808 an eminent surgeon, Henry Cline (1750-1827) purchased Bounds Green House (which stood to the south of today's Cline Road) and 69 acres of surrounding land and took up the lease on a further 143 acres of the Bowes Manor farmland. At this time Cline had succeeded his tutor, Thomas Smith, as lecturer and Surgeon at St Thomas's Hospital, and later became Master (1815) and President (1823) of the Royal College of Surgeons. Henry Cline lived in Lincoln's Inn Fields but his interest in farming led him to acquire Bounds Green House as his country seat. He was also a staunch Whig and supporter of radical causes, sympathetic to the French Revolution and supporter of the reforms proposed by John Thelwell and the Rev. J. Horne Tooke. According to Sir Astley Cooper, his friend and former pupil, Cline became more involved in politics and farming than in capitalising on his professional skills. He was succeeded at St Thomas's as Surgeon by his son, also Henry Cline (1775-1820).

In 1843 the farm, then comprising 276 acres of which only 11 acres of woodland remained, was occupied by Huntley Bacon, who lived in Bounds Green House. Bacon, later Lt. Col., came from a military family. The large house stood in about 50 acres surrounded by pleasure grounds, kitchen garden, plantation, pond, tennis court, coach houses and stables. The driveway was flanked with Lombardy poplar trees. The farm buildings stood to the north of today's Cline Road. At this time 176 acres of the farm was tenanted by Frederick Attenbring who was also renting 95 acres of Wood Green Farm at the same time.

The demise of the farm began a year or two before 1850 when the Great Northern Railway burrowed its Wood Green-New Southgate Tunnel under the middle of the farm and claimed about 6 acres of land at the north-west and south-eastern extremities for the tunnel approaches. The land above the tunnel was later leased by Wood Green Urban District Council (*c*.1910) to create Tunnel Gardens. By 1871 the Great Northern Railway had requisitioned some land to the south for the GNR Enfield Branch line from Wood Green station and by 1893 a large field at the north-western corner was leased to Friern Barnet UDC for the building of a sewage works and filter beds. The railways later secured more land on the south to expand their sidings north of Wood Green station.

In 1868 the farm was occupied by Charles Gould. The last farmer was Mrs Bayley, the daughter of Thomas Gould, who saw part of the farm (north of today's Cline Road) sold to erect a glassworks *c*.1910 (later the Standard Bottle Works). Other parts of the farm were let on building leases in 1913 and 1923. Bounds Green House was derelict by the early 1920s and the farmhouse was pulled down in 1927. Fields on the southern boundary bordering the Muswell Stream were acquired by the UDC to build an extension to Durnsford Road and to create the Albert Road Recreation Ground. Subsequently, two large fields on the west of the farm, were added to Muswell Hill Golf Course. A small parcel of the original woodland remains as Bluebell Wood and adjacent fields as allotments. The northernmost part of the former farmland is now occupied by the Bounds Green Industrial Estate and by part of the Middlesex University campus.

In 1843, 58 acres of the former Bowes Manor Farm on the east side of Bounds Green Road, between the northern boundary of Wood Green Farm and the parish of Edmonton, was leased by a Mr Calvert and tenanted by Thomas Holland. This land was sold along with Bowes Manor and eventually became Myddleton Road and the Bowes Park district.

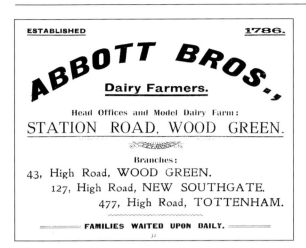

26. *Advertisement for the Abbott Brothers' Dairy Farm in Station Road. Their dairy became a United Dairies' depot by the 1930s. From the Wood Green Guide 1910.*

27. *Farm buildings in Mayes Lane c.1870. This became the site of Barratt's confectionery works.*

SMALLER FARMS

In 1843 Elm Lodge Farm to the north of Chapmans Green owned by William Hobson occupied 42 acres of meadow farmed by James Giblett. This farm survived to the beginning of the 20th century when its eastern flank was acquired by the London County Council for part of its White Hart Lane estate.

Two small farmsteads were located to the south of Wood Green Common. One of 25 acres to the south of Mayes Lane survived until 1870. In 1843 it was owned by Mary Weekley and farmed by Joshua Walker. The other, of 34 acres owned by Pagean Wright, was farmed by William Hayhow. Most of this area was to be later occupied by Barratt's Confectionery Works.

By the latter part of the 19th century dairy farms had been established to supply milk and other products. Andrews Dairy Farm based on Broadwater Farm, Tottenham, The Friern Manor Dairy Farm at Highgate and Tilstons at Stroud Green were amongst the larger of these. In Wood Green itself was Abbotts with its model dairy farm in Station Road and The Harringay Farm Dairy in Green Lanes.

28. *Chesser's blacksmith's at the junction of High Road and Lordship Lane in 1924. It was founded in 1770. Watercolour by J.E. Savery.*

From Hamlet to Village

Between 1619 and 1798 the population of Wood Green ward, which included West Green, increased from 50 to about 100 and retained the character of a scattered hamlet but towards the end of the 18th century this small hamlet had begun to expand. In 1770 George Chesser established his blacksmith's shop on the corner of High Road and Lordship Lane (later known as Spouters Corner) to take advantage of the increasing traffic. His smithy remained operational into the 1920s. Wood Green's first inn, the Three Jolly Butchers, located just north of today's bus garage, was licensed in 1781 in the name of Thomas King. It was a coaching inn with livery stables but it also catered for drovers en route to London. The Queen's Head inn on Green Lanes south of Ducketts Common opened in 1794 and the Nag's Head, opposite the smithy, was established by 1800.

By the turn of the nineteenth century there were several large houses around the common and a few were built as country seats by wealthy City people such as Wood Green House, Chitts Hill House and Bounds Green House. In 1818 a cluster of dwellings stood at the junction of the High Road, along the south side of what is now Station Road and several were scattered along Lordship Lane. Two cottages were built on Green Lanes near to Ducketts. The population between 1811 and 1841 grew to around 400 and the 1831 census recorded 123 inhabited houses in Wood Green ward with 22 being constructed. By 1837 there was a beerhouse in Station Road (then known as Wood Green Road) which later became the Jolly Anglers, a name that referred to the New River on the other side of the road. Nine cottages and two houses were built along Station Road adjacent to the pub. A row of these, Elm Cottages, survived until the 1930s.

The Watson family were the entrepreneurial proprietors of the Three Jolly Butchers for several decades from 1810. They also owned fields surrounding the inn and extending along Bounds

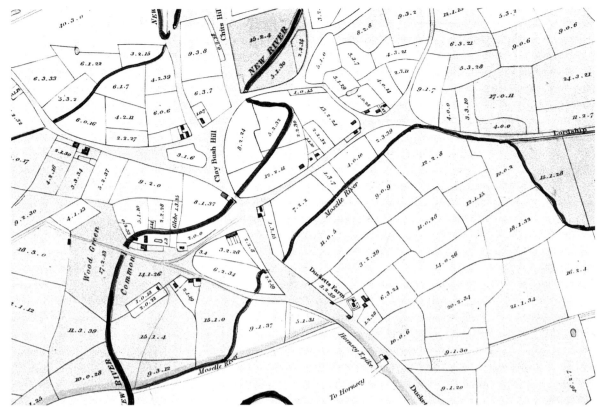

29. Extract from a map of the parish of Tottenham, 1818. Drawn by Johnathon and William Newton for Robinson's History and Antiquities of Tottenham, and based on a 1798 Survey. It shows little development since the map of 1619 (see p.14), except the disappearance of woodland. The field sizes are in acres, roods and perches.

Green Road. By 1843 four cottages had been built with others under construction; one of these also served as a police station. Two of the earliest (5-7 Bounds Green Road) are Grade II listed and are now the oldest surviving residential buildings in Wood Green. The Watsons also owned the land which became the site of the Printers' Almshouses. Their name is recorded for posterity in Watson's Road, once a cul de sac which ran behind the Three Jolly Butchers and in which ten houses were built by the Watsons before 1863; a post office also existed by this time.

The transformation of Wood Green from hamlet to village in the true sense was when it acquired its own church. Until 1844 the faithful made the journey to the parish church of All Hallows, near Bruce Castle, a distance of one and a half miles or more on unmade roads which were very muddy in bad weather. In that year a chapel-of-ease, seating 200, was built for Wood Green on common land at what was once known as the Roundabout, at the corner of the High Road and Bounds Green Road. The chapel, dedicated to St Michael, was designed by (Sir) George Gilbert Scott and W.B. Moffatt and consecrated on 3 October 1844. Services were conducted by clergy from All Hallows until 1862, when the Rev. John Thomas was appointed curate.

A plan of the parish of Tottenham published in 1844 shows the new ecclesiastical district of St Michael's and a rural scene with a developing village centre around the Wood Green Common and the High Road south of Bounds Green Road, together with scattered farmsteads. With the creation of the the ecclesiastical district the hamlet of West Green became detached from Wood Green. While the eastern, northern, and western boundaries of the new district were the same as for the ward, the southern boundary with the parish of Holy Trinity, Tottenham Green, followed that of Ducketts Farm.

30. Georgian houses in Bounds Green Road. Photograph 1997.

31. Wood Green Police Station, 1898. It stood on the corner of High Road and Nightingale Road.

KEEPING THE PEACE

One indication of the growth of Wood Green was the more sophisticated arrangements for policing the area.

From medieval times law and order in Tottenham manor was the responsibilities of constables appointed at annual manorial courts. and from 1515 a constable was appointed for Wood Green ward.

From 1750 this appointment passed to the parish vestry which was also responsible for the watch or night patrols. It would appear that by the 1830s Tottenham Vestry had become negligent in this matter, leading to a temporary constabulary being raised by public subscription.

This was not the only time that the populace at large was personally involved in law and order. At times of civil unrest local militia were sometimes recruited. This happened at the time of the French Revolution, when there were expressions of republicanism in Britain. At the time the Tottenham Loyal Association was formed and on 17 December 1792 the Vestry passed a resolution

> of support for the Constitution, Government and the House of Brunswick and to support the civil authority and if necessary in suppressing all Riots and Tumults and bring to justice the authors and promoters thereof

The resolution was signed by 69 ratepayers including several prominent Wood Green residents. The militia existed for four years but does not seem to have been particularly active.

In the meantime, the formation of the Bow Street Runners by Henry Fielding and his half-brother in 1749 had led to a more effective policing in the metropolis. Mounted patrols were also set up to police the turnpike roads up to a 20-mile radius of the capital. The no. 51 mounted patrol was stationed at Wood Green from 1805, its 'police station' being a house on Bounds Green Road rented from Alexander Watson, then proprietor of the Three Jolly Butchers. In 1840 the resident officer of the law was John Baker.

Under Sir Robert Peel's reforms, the Metropolitan Police were established in 1829 and the Bow Street patrols were integrated with them in 1836. In 1839 the Metropolitan Police area was extended to 15 miles from the City and Tottenham became 'Y' Division in which Wood Green's first police station was built in 1866 on the site of the present station on the High Road at the corner of Nightingale Road. In 1883 Wood Green was transferred to Hornsey Division. The police station was rebuilt and enlarged in 1908 and continues to serve the community today.

The Larger Houses

In 1664, when residents were taxed on the number of hearths in their houses, there were only three houses in Wood Green which had five or more hearths, and eight of either four or three hearths. The larger houses would have included those located around Wood Green Common in the 1619 Survey. These early houses or their 18th-century successors, such as Moat Cottage, Wood Green Cottage, The Grange and Cherson House, survived until the end of the 19th century. Other large houses were built by the end of the 18th century. These included Wood Green House (on the site of today's Alexandra House in Station Road), Elm Lodge (at Chapmans Green) and Bounds Green House.

Wood Green found favour with City gentlemen, merchants and traders as a convenient place to live. They could combine the benefits of rural living and yet be able to travel into the City on a daily basis if necessary. Their impact in terms of numbers and size of the buildings was modest compared with neighbouring Hornsey and Highgate or, indeed, Tottenham itself. The census of 1831 records 29 'capitalists, bankers, professionals' resident in the Wood Green Ward.

Some of the large houses and estates of Wood Green have been researched. Four of them are dealt with below.

NIGHTINGALE HALL

In 1715 the Woodreddings estate (*see* p.11), was acquired by George Wanley, a City goldsmith and landowner in Tottenham and elsewhere. In 1736 it passed to John Sawbridge, another prominent landowner in Tottenham and Edmonton. About this time there are references to a house and farmstead on the estate in the Tottenham court rolls, although the building may have been of Elizabethan origin. The house was known as Nightingale Hall in the latter half of the 18th century and the estate was of 72 acres during the tenure of John Giles, another Tottenham landowner. By the early part of the 19th century it had passed to the Woodward family who enlarged it to 88 acres with the acquisition of Dears Pightle and Bakersfield (*see* p11). As previously noted the farmland by this time was tenanted by Thomas Rhodes who owned the neighbouring Tottenham Wood Farm. In 1848 the Great Northern Railway acquired a strip of land running in a north-westerly direction through the middle of the estate with the result that by 1850 Thomas Rhodes was able to add 30 acres to the west of the railway to his farm. Thomas Pearson, a solicitor, who by this time was tenant at Nightingale Hall, acquired the Hall and land comprising 29 acres to the east of the railway, becoming the first owner to actually live there. The Pearson family, and particularly Mrs Pearson, were substantial property owners in Wood Green, and

32. Nightingale Hall, c.1892. The view is from the south west.

had an important influence on the development of Wood Green and St Michael's Church in particular. Following the death of her husband in 1862, the widow became Mrs Pearson-Kidd, her new husband being John Kidd, a printing ink manufacturer, who was active in local affairs and for some time was chairman of the Wood Green Ratepayers' Association. Mrs Pearson-Kidd, who died in 1891, was the last occupant at Nightingale Hall.

The Hall itself was on three floors, with seven bedrooms and an organ room. It underwent a Victorian Gothic face-lift in the latter half of the 19th century. A separate farmhouse, stables and outbuildings were adjacent and it had a well laid out garden (see 1864 O.S. Map). Further erosion of the estate resulted from the tunnelling of the amended route of the New River on the east flank (1852), expansion of the GNR railway lines to the west (1880) and the creation of the Palace Gates Station and GER line on the south (1878). A sale plan of 1891 shows that the estate was down to 10 acres. Nightingale Hall was demolished in 1894-5, but it is commemorated locally in the names of Nightingale Road, the Nightingale pub, Nightingale Gardens and Nightingale Primary School.

CHITTS HILL HOUSE

The Chitts Hill estate was bounded by the High Road on the west, Wolves Lane to the east,

Earlham Grove to the south and the parish boundary with Edmonton to the north. Chitts Hill was a local prominence of 120 feet above sea level, at the junction of today's Woodside Road and Cross Road which in Tudor times was common or waste land connected to both the high road and White Hart Lane by common lanes.

The land which became the Chitts Hill Estate was once part of a larger entity known as Belsars, part of the Bowes Manor Estate, which extended into the parish of Edmonton. This name derives from 'Belsiège' (*c.f.* Belsize) which means beautiful seat or place and has Norman origins. Belsars was a farm in the vicinity of Tottenhall Road (once known as Belsers Lane) but its exact location is not certain. Towards the end of the 17th century Belsars had become a separate freehold entity. During the 18th century it was owned by a succession of wealthy citizens including George Wanley, John Sawbridge and, interestingly, by Josiah Wedgwood the famous pottery maker as mortgagee in the sum of £1500 between 1785-95. In 1800 it was purchased by local landowner William Wrangham for £3000 and following his death was sold to a City oil merchant, James Clark in 1805. Chitts Hill House, a fine bow-fronted Regency building, was built for him *c.*1805-6 near the top of Chitts Hill, with views over the New River to both the west and the south, with a carriage drive from the high road.

33. *Chitts Hill House, an undated photograph. The view is from the north west.*

34. The former gatehouse to Chitts Hill House, c.1910, then tea rooms.

The Quaker Banker

After Clark's death in 1815 the estate of 31 acres was bought by the Quaker banker John Overend (1769-1832). He founded the firm of Richardson, Overend & Co. in 1805 which in 1830 became Overend, Gurney & Co. the discount bankers. The firm became notorious for its collapse in 1866, which brought about a disastrous run on other London banks, but during Overend's lifetime was spectacularly successful. He had the circular gatehouse built at the entrance to his carriage drive in 1822 and it survives today, known as the 'Roundhouse' or 'Mushroom House', at the corner of Woodside Road. It is one of Wood Green's oldest buildings and is Grade II listed. The gatehouse was the residence of the gatekeeper or coachman and in 1871 was occupied by the coachman, his wife, six children *and* a lodger! Overend was survived by his second wife Mary (1783-1862), a very wealthy lady, who was known for her benevolence and kindness and who established a local charity which today supports the residents of Forster's Almshouses in Philip Lane, Tottenham. The Overends' estate attracted the attention of Keane in his *Beauties of Middlesex* (1850) who wrote:

> Chitshill - The seat of Mrs Overend is contiguous to Bowes Manor. The house is seated on rising ground and is approached by a winding carriage drive from a pretty Gothic lodge on the right hand side of the high road to Southgate. At a short distance from the house is a span-roof conservatory surrounded by pleasure grounds, and in front flows the New River spanned by a pretty Gothic bridge.

35. John Overend (1769-1832). Etching by Richard Dighton, 1822.

The City Tea Dealer

Samuel Page (1810-1886), a City tea dealer, purchased the estate from Mary Overend's executors in 1863. By this time it totalled 48 acres and the house and surroundings were well established and the fields rented to local farmers.

Page extended the house and won some acclaim in horticultural circles in 1876 for a new conservatory he added to the house. He was a substantial benefactor to St Michael's and, with his first wife, supported its rebuilding in 1863-64. He also bore the cost of the tower, spire, clock and the peal of six bells in 1873-74 in memory of his first wife.

In 1875 the estate was extended to include the neighbouring Westbury House (later Earlham Grove House). The Page family left Chitts Hill House in 1881 and the estate was sold to the Freehold Cottage Dwelling Co. Ltd. By 1893 it was surrounded by the new roads of the Chitts Hill Park Estate and itself was demolished between 1895-1900 to be replaced by Sylvan Avenue.

36. *Westbury House c.1870. Later known as Earlham Grove House and now as Woodside House.*

WESTBURY HOUSE (later EARLHAM GROVE HOUSE)

The East India Merchant

Other merchants seeking rural retreats were the former agents of the East India Company who returned to Britain following the Indian Mutiny and the subsequent replacement of that Company by Crown control in 1858. Typical of these was Thomas William Smith Oakes (1826-1906), a native of Swaffham, Norfolk, who had established himself as an East India merchant in the City. In 1863-4 he bought ten acres of land which today forms most of Woodside Park. Here, he built a solid residence in the Italianate Style known as Westbury House, where he lived with his wife and ten children in some style. One of Oakes's daughters, Marie Emilie, later Mrs Shaw, wrote down her recollections of Wood Green and the house as it was during her schooldays, in her memoirs written in 1945:

> I was about six or seven, when we moved to Wood Green, which was then a straggling village with gentlemen's estates around. My Father bought land and built a large family house for us. Although a pukka City man, he loved the country. We had 3 cows, pigs, poultry, dogs etc., and always a horse or two. The stables and outhouses were spacious and airy and much beloved by my brothers and self as

a playground. The rooms over the harness room and other buildings were occupied by the gardener and his wife ...

> We had a resident governess for a time, and a nice bright school room on the second floor but I don't remember learning anything from the two we had, and eventually I was sent to a large day-school, not far from us.

Mrs Shaw also describes Westbury House as follows:

> This was a typical Victorian building, a huge block, perforated with windows, mostly bow on the ground and first floor. An imposing portico over the front entrance between the dining-room and lower drawing-room. To the right a conservatory (in which the family designed and laid a mosaic floor) and then another front door, or rather side door, leading into a tiled vestibule and billiard-room with its own dressing room and lavatory, thus friends of father's could come and have their games without in any way interfering with the rest of the house ... The central hall was very big, with a large fire-place,-doors all around. The kitchen premises were shut off at the end. Eight rooms, bathroom, lavatory on the 1st floor: one room was the upper drawing-room, about the same size as the one below, with the

37. Mrs Emilie Oakes (1835-1918), Wife of Thomas William Smith Oakes lived at Westbury House 1865-73.

38. Mrs Catherine Smithies, campaigner for Temperance and animal welfare, lived at Earlham Grove House.

same large crystal chandelier beloved of the Victorians!! On the floor above were the nurseries and other bedrooms, bathrooms and lavatories on each floor.

There was a back staircase leading from the servants' bedrooms down to the kitchen, pantries etc. Back doors led to the stable-yard, tradesmen's doors etc.. This yard was closed with big gates, and a smaller gate opposite led into the kitchen garden and orchard.

The Oakes family lived at Westbury House until 1874 when Thomas Oakes sold up as a result of business difficulties and moved to more modest accommodation in Holloway. In 1875 the property, by this time known as Earlham Grove House, became part of the Chitts Hill estate.

The Campaigning Family

The next occupants were the Smithies family, well known for their Christian philanthropy and support for the Temperance movement. Mrs Catherine Smithies (1785-1877) was a vigorous campaigner for Temperance and animal welfare.

She founded the Band of Mercy movement, a charitable organisation for young people aimed at relieving the suffering of animals, which subsequently became part of the RSPCA. Following her death in 1877, her son organised a public subscription to erect an obelisk to his mother's memory. It was unveiled in 1879 on the south side of Bounds Green Road but was relocated to the north side to enable tramway lines to be laid. It stands today as one of Wood Green's landmarks, situated in Bounds Green Road, ironically facing the Prince of Wales pub.

Thomas Bywaters Smithies, her son, (1816-1883) championed similar causes but also supported the struggles of the working man. He was the proprietor of many philanthropic journals including *The British Workman, The Family Friend, The Child's Companion, Friendly Greetings*, as well those concerned with temperance and animal welfare such as *The Band of Hope Review, Our Four-footed Friends,* and *Our Dumb Companions*.

Smithies died on 26 July 1883 and was buried at Abney Park Cemetery in Stoke Newington where his mother was also buried. The following

39. *The obelisk to commemorate Mrs Catherine Smithies arrives in Bounds Green Road in 1879. St Michael's Church and school are to the right and the rear of the Fishmongers' Almshouses to the left.*

eulogy was given by the minister of the Wood Green Presbyterian Church at his funeral:

> He will be mourned by thousands today. The poor and sick in our own neighbourhood especially will miss him. There will be many a sad heart among the soldiers and cabmen and railwaymen in whom he took so deep an interest … and when Thomas Smithies died last Friday the working men of England lost one of their best friends.

In 1881 Earlham Grove House was sold as part of the Chitts Hill Estate to the Freehold House Property Co. Ltd. Shortly after it passed into municipal ownership which has allowed its survival to the present day as an example of one of Wood Green's larger 19th-century residences.

40. *The obelisk in its original position at the corner of Park Avenue in 1904.*

41. *Thomas Bywaters Smithies (1817-1883), publisher and campaigner for Temperance and the welfare of the Working Man. He lived at Earlham Grove House.*

42. *Brabançonne Villa, c.1930. Then the Providence Convent, it stood at the corner of Earlham Grove and High Road.*

BRABANÇONNE VILLA
The Local Dignitary
Brabançonne Villa stood on the southern corner of Earlham Grove and the High Road opposite the present police station. Built in 1870 for James Coleman, a business associate of Thomas Oakes of nearby Westbury House, it originally stood in half an acre of land. It was bought in 1871 by Alfred Durrant (1839-1899), another East India merchant, who had resided for a few years previously in the newly built Pellatt Grove. He added an extra half-acre to the grounds. It was the home of the Durrant family for the next fifty years. They had seven children in all, five being born in Wood Green. During their occupation the house became surrounded by mature plantings with a lawn and tennis court and an orchard to the rear.

In 1873 Durrant purchased the remaining land on the south side of Earlham Grove and from 1885 leased plots for building Nos 1-14 Earlham Grove which remain today. As well as being a successful business man and property owner Durrant was an important Wood Green politician and dignitary. Colonel Durrant, as he was known on account of honorary rank bestowed by the Honourable Artillery Corps, was of Lib-

eral persuasion. He sat on the Tottenham Board of Health and School Board, becoming chairman of the latter in 1891, and was a Justice of the Peace. He played a prominent part in the campaign for the administrative separation of Wood Green from Tottenham which was fulfilled in 1888. He was an active churchgoer and became a regular worshipper at St Mark's, Noel Park, after its opening in 1889 although technically he was a parishioner of St Michael's, Wood Green. He played an active part in the campaign to establish the Passmore Edwards (later the Wood Green) Cottage Hospital and also in the Pleasant Sunday Afternoon (PSA) Movement and was a trustee of many charities. Durrant died on 28 October 1899 and was buried in Highgate Cemetery. At his funeral his Vicar said:

> The Cottage Hospital would ever be a monument of Col. Durrant's anxiety for the welfare of the suffering poor and of his unstinting energy. He wore himself out in the public service.

Mrs Durrant and her children remained at Brabançonne Villa until her death in 1920.

The Convent
In 1921 the villa was to have a new lease of life when it was purchased by the Daughters of Providence to use as a senior school for their Providence Convent School, then in Stuart Crescent. A new school building was erected in 1926 on the site of the orchard to the rear of the house in Earlham Grove, which housed both junior and senior schools and La Brabançonne became the Providence Convent until 1933 when the Sisters moved to a new convent in Oakthorpe Road, Palmers Green. The house was sold in 1938 and was in commercial use, except for ARP requisition during World War Two, until it was acquired by the local authority in 1965. It was demolished in the early 1970s to make way for council housing. The school was closed in 1975 when the pupils were transferred to St Angela's Roman Catholic School for Girls in Palmers Green. The school building subsequently became the Cypriot Community Centre which it remains today.

The Early Railways

43. *Wood Green Great Northern station in Station Road in 1899.*

44. *Railways into Wood Green c.1900. In 1878 the Great Eastern line to Palace Gates station was constructed across the then unbuilt Noel Park estate, with another station called Green Lanes by the time of this map. This line was closed in 1964.*

The tranquility of Wood Green was disturbed in the mid-19th century with the coming of the railways. The first line, which ran through the east side of the parish of Tottenham, was the Northern and Eastern Railway from Stratford to Broxbourne. This opened in 1840 with a station at Tottenham (later known as Tottenham Hale) and a further station called Marsh Lane (later Park Lane and ultimately Northumberland Park) was added in 1842. This line had little or no impact on Wood Green, being situated at least two miles to the east, but probably encouraged early residential occupation of the West Green area.

The Great Northern Railway Act of 1846 was to be much more significant. The line opened in 1850 running initially from Maiden Lane near King's Cross with stations at Hornsey and Colney Hatch (later New Southgate). It ran directly north

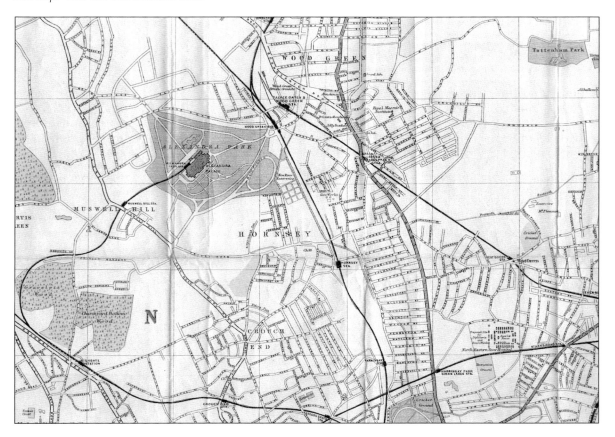

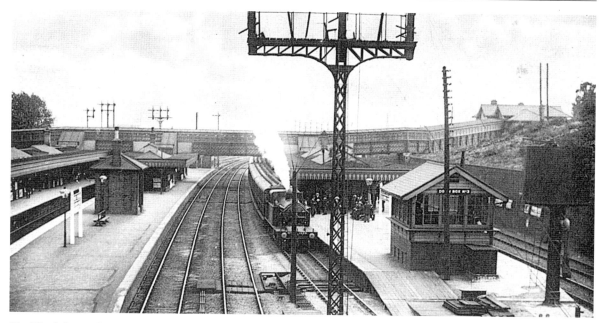

45. *Wood Green Great Northern station in 1905. By this time the footbridge connected booking offices on both sides of the tracks with the platforms.*

through the middle of Wood Green traversing the western side of Wood Green Common, bisecting the Nightingale Hall estate, and passing under Bounds Green in a tunnel to New Southgate and beyond. A sum of £4,000 towards the cost of a station at Wood Green was contributed by the Rhodes family of the adjacent Tottenham Wood Farm, who saw the potential of its land for building. The station, named Wood Green, was opened in 1859 with two platforms and a booking office on the down side. This line provided easy access to London for residents, local produce and goods, and was a stimulus for residential development of the area. With the opening of Alexandra Park in 1863, the station became Wood Green (Alexandra Park), reverting to Wood Green in 1971. Its present name of Alexandra Palace was introduced in 1982.

In 1871 the Great Northern Railway opened a branch line from Wood Green to Enfield creating a loop to the north of Wood Green station. Bowes Park station was opened in 1880 to cater for the needs of that expanding area.

The earliest plans for Alexandra Palace made provision for a branch of the Great Northern Railway from Highgate to the Palace itself. This line, incorporating a short section of the Muswell Hill Railway (within the Palace grounds) was opened on 24 May 1873 with an intermediate

station at Muswell Hill. The line was closed as a result of the first Palace fire and reopened on 1 May 1875. With the growth of Muswell Hill a second intermediate station was opened at Cranley Gardens in 1902. In its early days the line's ups and downs paralleled that of the Palace and later it suffered severe competition from tramways, buses and ultimately the Underground. The line was closed to passenger traffic on 3 July 1954.

In 1878 the Great Eastern Railway built a branch line from Seven Sisters terminating at Palace Gates, a station at the junction of today's Bridge Road and Dorset Road, only a few hundred yards from the Wood Green GNR station. This branch had intermediate stations at West Green and Green Lanes (renamed Noel Park and Wood Green in 1902). The Palace Gates line also had an important influence on the residential development of Wood Green because it allowed workers to travel to the docks and factories of east London.

The GNR and GER lines became part of the London & North Eastern Railway after the First World War.

A scheme proposed as early as 1866 to make a connection between the GER line and GNR lines to the north of Wood Green station was never implemented. However, a single-track

connection, just north of Palace Gates Station was made between the Palace Gates line and the Enfield branch line in 1929, which was used for excursion trips in the 1930s and was upgraded during the last war for strategic purposes. However, soon after its inception the Palace Gates branch faced competition from trams, and from 1932 the Underground. In the post-war years its viability remained problematical and it was a victim of Dr Beeching's cuts in 1962. The last passenger service was on 5 January 1963 and the last freight was carried in December 1964.

The triangle of land between the old GNR main line and the closed Palace Gates terminus, north of Wood Green station, was used to service British Rail's Inter-City trains, known as the Bounds Green Depot, in the late 1970s. This land once formed the southernmost part of Bounds Green Farm.

46. *(Top) Palace Gates (GER) station in 1902.*

47. *(Centre) The entrance to Palace Gates (LNER) station in Bridge Road, c.1960.*

48. *(Below) Noel Park Great Eastern (later LNER) station c.1910.*

Residential Development

VICTORIAN VILLAS

The arrival of the Great Northern Railway and its stations in 1850 and 1859 (*see* pp44-45) encouraged development which, until its arrival, had hardly taken place beyond the village centre.

The first expansion, away from Wood Green Common and the junction of High Road and Bounds Green Road (then called Jolly Butchers Hill), was of a number of large villas built from the early 1860s along the east side of the High Road. These appear on the 1864 O.S. Map. In 1862 a property developer, Thomas Clark, built

'12 pairs of houses' known as Dovecote Villas, on the east side of the High Road south of Ducketts farmhouse. They were two-and three-storey semi-detached villas with large gardens fronting the road. Similar houses were built opposite Ducketts Common and more on the east side towards St Ann's Road. Further north, on the west side, stood The Elms, opposite Lordship Lane, a detached house in its own grounds, and Alma, Crimea and Southgate Villas were built opposite what is now Woodside Park. Southgate Villa was a good example of a substantial house of the mid-Victorian period. Described as a detached family residence, it stood on the corner of Truro Road and the High Road. Set back from the highway it featured: a portico reached by a flight of steps; a 25 ft x 9 ft entrance hall; a 27 ft x 15 ft dining room; a 41 ft by 15 ft drawing room and ten bedrooms. Its grounds included:

49. Extract from the 1864 OS map, showing the early development of Wood Green.

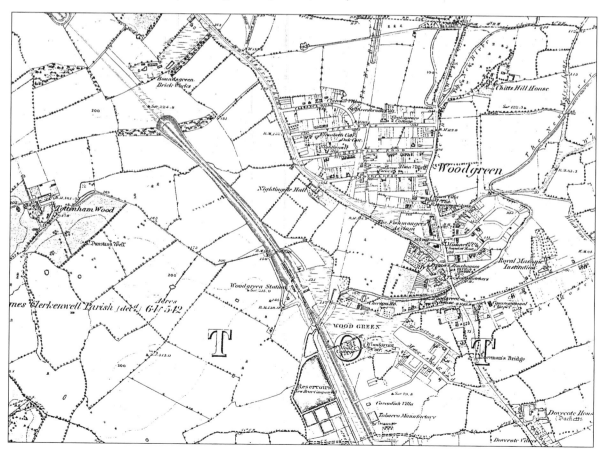

50. *The Elms, High Road, c.1900. It was on the site of Broadway Parade and the Gaumont.*

'Asphalted and Gravelled Walks, Croquet Lawn, Flower Beds, Fancy Rockery, Fountains, Fruit and Vegetable Gardens.' The gardens included 'Peach Houses, A Range of Vineries, Propagating, Cucumber and Greenhouses, Potting House and Excellent Poultry Yards.'

In 1879 it was rented at £75 per annum, then a significant sum, and put up for sale in 1880. The site was subsequently redeveloped with more modest properties. Though some of the large houses, like Southgate Villa, did not survive much more than thirty years, some large detached houses were still being built well into the latter half of the 19th century and included Westbury House (1865), Brabançonne Villa (1870) and The Mansion (in Alexandra Park Road) (*c*.1870).

By 1864 several similar villas had been built along the south side of Lordship Lane. But, with the exception of the Hornsey Turnpike house and the Queen's Head inn, no houses had yet been built on the west side of Green Lanes between Turnpike Lane and the Manor House.

VICTORIAN ESTATES

Even before Wood Green station opened in 1859, building societies had acquired farmland in the area. The first major plan in 1853 described the 'Wood Green Estate, Middlesex, purchased by the Finsbury Freehold Land Society for distribution amongst its members'. These 92 acres comprised the larger part of Wood Green Farm in an inverted triangle between the High Road and Bounds Green Road to the north of St Michael's Church. The farm was sold by James Foster during

51. *The Mansion, Alexandra Park Road c.1939. Demolished in 1960, it was replaced by Anderton Court.*

1852 and 1853 in two parts to Charles Paul Millard and Robert Warner respectively, who in turn sold them to the Society. Millard, a City tea dealer, later owned the Bounds Green Pottery and Tile Works.

The Society's development described 480 plots west of the High Road and eventually included Commerce, Nightingale, Finsbury, Truro and Clarence Roads. The first plots were sold early in 1855. Standard plots 160 x 36 ft were offered at £34 with larger ones at £37+ per annum. A good standard of development was ensured by the fact that house ownership above a certain rateable value gave a right to vote. This was the reason for the presence of land societies with political affiliations, such as the National Liberal Land Company and the Conservative Land Society.

In 1851 the population of Wood Green ward was 1259 but by 1861, after the opening of Wood Green Station, it had risen to 3154 occupying 565 houses. These figures included the area around West Green, then within the Wood Green ward, which had grown rapidly with some well-developed streets such as Summerhill Road, Philip Lane and St Ann's Road; one of the principal developers here was Edward Clarke, a builder, of West Green.

The OS Map of 1864 shows houses on the Wood Green Estate and also a number in Stuart Crescent and Ewart and Pellatt Groves to the east of

52. *Truro Road, c.1905.*

the High Road. To the south the Economic Free-hold Land Society offered plots in Mayes Road and Caxton Road in 1863; some of the existing houses date from that time. The larger houses were detached or semi-detached, attractive to the aspiring middle classes whilst others took the form of spacious cottages. Examples of this mixed type of development, built by local firms, can still be seen in these roads today. The late Victorian terrace had not yet arrived.

William Spencer Clarke in his *Suburban Houses of London - A residential guide* (1881) said:

> From the site of the Hornsey turnpike to the north-west are capital detached villas [Dove-cote Villas] and to the left Mayes Road, Caxton Road and others, ranging from £40 to £70 rental and Wood Green has now become almost an independent colony.

TERRACES

Acacia and Winkfield Roads, on the north side of Lordship Lane, were laid out by 1864 and occupation of the slightly higher density ter-raced housing here began in 1876. To the north, the Newnham Road and Canning Crescent area was planned by the Conservative Land Society in 1865 and residents were living in Newnham Road by 1868.

Kelly's *Post Office Directory* in 1868 notes that there were 323 'private residents' or household-ers and shopkeepers (excluding tenants), whereas

four years later it recorded 545. In 1869, 10 acres of freehold building land in Wood Green could be bought for £4500, a freehold detached villa with nine rooms for about £900, and a similar semi-detached property for £700. A detached house in Truro Road could be rented at £36 per annum. By 1871 the overall population had risen to 5011.

The district of Bowes Park, lying between the GNR railway and the High Road and between Clarence Road and Bowes Road, was built on the southern part of the Bowes Farm Manor Estate from the 1870s. The expansion of this northern

53. *Buckingham Road c.1905, showing the premises of W. Parker, jobmaster at Wood Green station.*

part of Wood Green was a consequence of the opening of the GNR branch line from Wood Green to Enfield in 1871, which in turn led to a station at Bowes Park in 1880.

In 1880 the Bowes Park Estate was auctioned for 'Persons seeking Rural and Salubrious Residences'. This initially comprised the High Road, Lascotts, Myddleton, Marquis and Parkhurst Roads, but encouraged by the National Liberal Land Company the development was extended to include Whittington, Palmerston, and Sidney Roads. By 1893 the Bowes Park district extended to the west of the railway to include Brownlow Road and Maidstone Road. In 1920 the chronicler, Thomas Burke, was moved to say:

> Bowes Park is Wood Green with its Sunday clothes on. Wood Green is the original Jack Jones; Bowes Park is Jack Jones 'come into a little bit o' splosh.'

The opening of the Great Eastern Railway branch line from Seven Sisters in 1878, with a station at Green Lanes (later Noel Park and Wood Green) terminating at Palace Gates, stimulated yet more development. The area south of Mayes Road to the Hornsey boundary, developed by the British Land Company Ltd as the Park Ridings Estate from the early 1880s, included Hornsey Park Road, Park Ridings, Alexandra Road and Brampton Park Road. The developer specified that the houses should be valued at not less than £300 or £350 depending on location. This was probably the first example of higher density late Victorian terraced housing in Wood Green, an earlier, more exotic, plan for this area involving large public gardens and a church having been set aside.

By 1881 the population had reached 9381.

THE NOEL PARK ESTATE

There was a need for cheaper accommodation for working class families some of whose breadwinners, working in the factories and docks of east London, could take advantage of the early workmen's tickets offered by the GER. In the absence of local authority provision at that time the need was met by the Artisans, Labourers and

54. *An advertising postcard for the Noel Park Estate.*

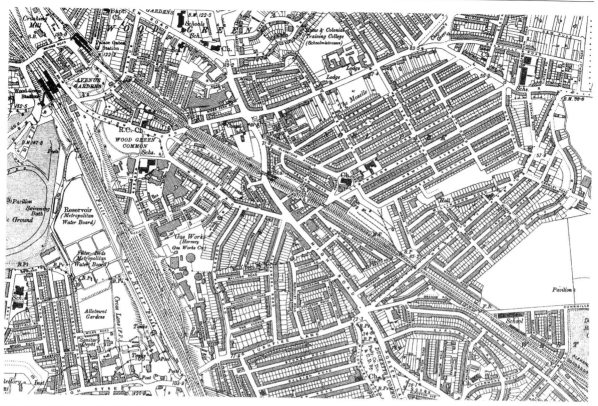

55. *The OS map of 1920, showing on the right hand side the extent of the Noel Park Estate east of the High Road.*

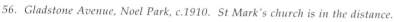

56. *Gladstone Avenue, Noel Park, c.1910. St Mark's church is in the distance.*

General Dwellings Company (AL&GD Co), which had been founded in 1867 by William Austin, a builder, to provide low-cost housing for the families of clerks and workmen. In 1881 the company bought 100 acres of the former Ducketts Farm, to the east of the High Road bounded by Westbury Avenue on the south and Lordship Lane to the north. This became the Noel Park Estate (named after Ernest Noel MP, chairman of the AL&GD Co.) which was laid out by the architect Roland Plumbe, from 1883. Five types of red-brick terraced houses with gardens were offered. They varied from four to eight rooms and were let from 5/9d to 12/6d weekly; maisonettes for two families from 5/- and 8/6d weekly. By 1893 the north side of Gladstone Avenue, Farrant, Moselle and Morley Avenues and part of Pelham Road were occupied. The south side of Gladstone Avenue and the roads to the north of Westbury Avenue were completed by 1907. The houses to the north between Moselle Avenue and Lordship Lane were completed by 1927.

On completion, the Noel Park Estate contained 2000+ houses, with a density of 27 houses per acre, and included the Cheapside shopping parade on the east of the High Road, built in 1911, and the Empire theatre, which replaced part of the mid-Victorian Dovecote Villas.

CONSOLIDATION

Plans were drawn up for the Tottenham Wood Estate on the former Tottenham Wood Farm as early as 1858, offering 91 sizeable building plots and new roads, but this scheme did not materialise due to the creation of Alexandra Park, which included the projected site, in 1863. By 1884 the Alexandra Estate, comprising Alexandra Park, Albert, Crescent and Victoria Roads, on part of the old Nightingale Hall Farm were laid out and partially built upon. After 1900 this estate was complete and roads to the north-west of Alexandra Park, such as The Avenue, Grove Avenue, Rosebery and Vallance Roads were developed on the former Alexandra Park land which

57. *Chitts Hill Park Estate, sales advertisement. From the Wood Green Guide, 1910.*

Chitts Hill Park Estate,

═══ WOOD GREEN, N. ═══

Six minutes from Bowes Park Station (G.N.R.), adjoining the Recreation Grounds of the Wood Green District Council. Within easy distance of the City or West End, by Train, Tube, or Tram (a Station of the latter being on the Estate).

Substantially Built Semi=detached Houses
FOR SALE or TO BE LET.

The Estate is situated on gentle rising ground of the Northern Heights, and is intersected by four tree-planted Avenues, which have been made up and taken over by the District Council, and are flanked by single and double-fronted high-class Villa Residences, containing from three to six bedrooms, two and three reception rooms, and all modern improvements.

Rents from £32 to £50 per annum.
Leasehold from £335 to £550.——
Ground Rents Moderate.   Freehold if desired.

Leases are for the full term of 99 years, and special facilities are afforded to public officials and other responsible persons for purchasing their houses on prolonged terms of payment.

High-class Flats in Double-Fronted Houses
AT VERY MODERATE RENTALS.

All seeking Residences in a healthy and good class locality are invited to visit the Estate before deciding elsewhere.

Wood Green is becoming a very important educational centre, and will be increasingly so when the proposed Secondary School is erected. Other attractions are the new Public Library, and the near proximity of the Alexandra Palace (about 20 minutes' walk).

58. Arcadian Gardens, Chitts Hill, c.1905.

59. Nightingale Hall Estate sales advertisement. From Wood Green Guide, 1910.

had been sold by the trustees to offset financial losses.

In 1881, the first part of the Chitts Hill Estate, a strip on the northern boundary lying between the High Road and Wolves Lane, was sold for building and became Lyndhurst Road. Later in the same year the remainder of the estate was sold to the Freehold Cottage Dwelling Company Ltd and by 1890 Woodside and Maryland Roads and Arcadian Villas (later Gardens) were laid out as the Chitts Hill Park Estate. In 1910 properties on this estate described as 'single and double-fronted high class Villa Residences, containing three to six bedrooms, two and three reception rooms, and all modern improvements' could be rented from £32 to £50 per annum or purchased leasehold for £335 to £550. Maisonettes were also available from 9/- to 12/6d weekly.

Development on the south of Bounds Green Road did not take place until after the demolition of Nightingale Hall in 1894-5. Building plans for the site existed in 1893 but these were set aside

NIGHTINGALE HALL ESTATE,
WOOD GREEN, N.

CORNER OF BRAEMAR AVENUE.

THE Nightingale Hall Estate (braemar, Cornwall, and Northcott Avenues, near Wood Green and Palace Gates Stations and the new Electric Trams, has been recently developed by J. H. James, with most conveniently planned Villas, from **£30** per Annum; and at Chitts Hill Park with well-arranged Maisonettes, from **9/-** to **12/6** weekly, and Villas at **£30** per annum. Wood Green, which is considered the healthiest suburb in London, with its Open Spaces for Recreation, Public Institutions, and great Educational advantages, has become a very desirable district in which to reside. All seeking accommodation from **9/-** per week to **£50** per annum should first of all apply by letter to—

J. H. JAMES (Owner), 6, Braemar Avenue.

60. Dorset Road c.1907, backing on to Palace Gates Station, built as cottages for railway workers.

in favour of the building of the Wood Green Cycling Track in 1895. However, five years later cycle racing gave way to development with the building of the terraces of the Nightingale Hall Estate – Imperial and Eastern Roads (1901-2), Northcott, Cornwall and Braemar Avenues (1907). Here, 'most conveniently planned Villas' were available from £30 per annum.

With the exception of the Noel Park estate housing developments in Wood Green up to the late 19th century were on a modest scale unlike the large estates of James Edmondson and J.C. Hill in neighbouring Hornsey. Generally, it was carried out by local builders such as James Pocock, J.H. James, William Styles, George Whymark and the like.

Larger scale developments on the southern fringes of the Wood Green area, on the west side of Green Lanes, later known as the 'Harringay Ladder', began in the late 1880s, initiated by the sale of the Harringay House estate to William Hodson of Dalston. He sold 91 acres, between today's Wightman Road and Green Lanes, to the British Land Co. in 1881. The major part of the Harringay House estate lay in Hornsey but the eastern ends of the roads forming 'the Ladder' lay at that time in Wood Green ward. The Harringay Park Estate, as the development was known, was completed by the turn of the 20th century.

The land to the east of Green Lanes between St Ann's Road and the Tottenham & Hampstead Junction Railway with its station at Harringay was developed by J.C. Hill in the late 1890s. John Cathles Hill (1857-1915) was a major developer in north London at that time with the Rathcoole Estate, Hornsey and the Broadway Parade, Crouch End amongst his other notable achievements. His development, known as 'The Gardens', included the Grand Parade of shops and the elaborate Salisbury Hotel in Green Lanes.

By the turn of the 20th century development of the area north of Lordship Lane around Chapmans Green had begun on the site of the former Elm Lodge Farm, centred initially on the triangle formed by Dunbar and Perth Roads. These new roads with Scottish names formed, not surprisingly, the 'Scotch Estate' later extending east to the area based on Eldon and Granville Roads. This estate was completed by the early 1920s.

Bounds Green still remained a rural hamlet, comprising Bounds Green House, some cottages and the Ranelagh Tavern until the late 1880s, when Brownlow and Maidstone Roads were built. Development to the south of the Bounds Green Road awaited the demise of the Bounds Green Farm in the 1920s.

By 1911 the population had reached 49,372 and in 1913 there were 10,249 houses.

MUNICIPAL EXPANSION

Up to 1920 large areas to the east, north and south of White Hart Lane, and in the north-west to the south of Bounds Green remained rural.

In 1920 Wood Green Urban District Council purchased or leased 51 acres of land to the north of Durnsford Road, once part of Bounds Green Farm, for housing development. The UDC's first council house was handed over on 26 July 1921, one of fifty houses on the Bounds Green Estate, on the north side of Durnsford Road. It was a cottage estate, part of the 'Homes for Heroes' scheme after the 1st World War, designed by T.H. Mawson and R. Daw.

The London County Council acquired 200 acres of farmland in Tottenham and Wood Green in 1901 but the building of its distinctive White Hart Lane cottage estate did not begin until 1920. It was to have included part of Wood Green to the south of White Hart Lane between today's Roundway and Berwick Road, but in 1921 Wood Green UDC purchased 29 acres of the land between Gospatrick Road and Berwick Road, from the LCC. On some of this the UDC built its second housing estate, the White Hart Lane Estate, between 1925-28, consisting of 190 houses in Crossway, James Gardens and Croxford Gardens with another 18 in Perth Road by 1931. These were designed by the Borough Engineer and Architect, C. H. Croxford, and built by local builders Rowley and Sons. This estate was contiguous with the LCC scheme. The weekly rental for a 3-bedroom house in 1931 was 12/7d, and 16/2d for 4 bedrooms. The remainder of the former LCC land became allotments and playing fields and later part became the site of Wood Green Comprehensive School.

In 1931 the population reached 54,181. By the outbreak of the Second World War, Wood Green's council housing stock totalled 261 houses.

POST-WAR EXPANSION

By 1949, 60 more council houses had been built at Bounds Green (Tunnel Gardens, Durnsford Road, Park Grove) and also 18 flats at Park Court. In the same year starts were made on houses and flats in Bounds Green Road (Bounds Green Court, The Hollies, and Woodfield House), Marlborough Road, Palmerston Road (Grasmere Court), Pellatt Grove (Greenwood House), Truro Road (Marlow House) and Vincent Road (Vincent Square). Some of these replaced war-damaged properties. The larger scale development of flats began in the

61. *Bounds Green Court, 1951.*

62. *Commerce Road, the old and the new, 1962.*

mid-1950s with Barnes Court (Clarence Road), Ellenborough Court (Ellenborough Road), Irving Court (Eldon Road), Corbett Court (Bounds Green Road), Granville Road and Bolster Grove (in Crescent Rise) completed in 1957.

In the late 1950s some of the original Victorian housing stock had deteriorated and major re-development schemes were put in hand at Winkfield and Acacia Roads, Edith Road and Pellatt Grove, the latter culminating in Progress Way by the end of the 1960s.

The first phase of the Commerce Road Redevelopment Scheme was inaugurated on 7 April 1962 by Sir Basil Spence. This was the last major building project carried out by Wood Green Council's Borough Engineer, A.J. Rebbeck. It provided 670 dwellings in four 15-storey blocks in Commerce Road, replacing houses and shops built one hundred years earlier. Part of this scheme involved re-locating some small manufacturers to the Bounds Green Industrial Estate.

At the time of the demise of Wood Green Council in 1965 almost 1500 council dwellings had been built. In 1965 the rents for council houses varied from 23/5d to 38/- and for flats from 22/6d to 42/6d.

63. *Edwards Cottages, off Commerce Road, prior to demolition, c.1960.*

64. *The architect, Basil Spence, with the mayor, Alderman A.G. Kendall, and Mrs Joyce Butler MP, at the inauguration of the Commerce Road Development Scheme on 7 April 1962.*

65. *St Michael's Chapel of Ease, erected in 1844. This was Wood Green's first church, which was enlarged in 1865. Lithograph by G. Hawkins.*

Wood Green Churches

A PARISH OF ITS OWN

In 1866 the ecclesiastical parish of St Michael's, Wood Green, was established, having been carved out of that of All Hallows, Tottenham. It had a population of 3,500. The first Vicar was the Rev. John Thomas, who had conducted services in Wood Green as curate from All Hallows since 1862 and was to remain incumbent for 45 years. He played an influential role in the rebuilding of the church and creating the fabric of the parish.

The site chosen for St Michael's Chapel of Ease at the junction of High Road and Bounds Green Road was a prominent one, but it became problematical on account of subsidence. This, coupled with the rapidly increasing population, soon required the church to be rebuilt. The first stage was a new nave designed by Henry Curzon (1865), a chancel (1871), and a tower and spire in 1874. The enlargement and conversion of the Sunday School, opened in 1859, into an Infants' day school was completed in 1863, with further

extension in 1886. St Michael's National Senior School, on the opposite side of Bounds Green Road, was opened in 1872. The rectory, also in the Bounds Green Road, was built in 1882.

The next incumbent, Rev. C.G.A. Midwinter, placed great emphasis on establishing parish institutions including building the Parish Hall, designed by J.S. Alder and which opened on 13 May 1911. Fr. Midwinter encouraged the formation of many church groups for young and old alike. Unfortunately, he also had to deal with further structural problems of the church, arising from the underlying clay, in 1908 and 1912. These have persisted to recent years with major repairs in the 1950s and again in 1992.

As the population increased six new parishes were created and two mission churches established within the original St Michael's parish boundary. The first was St Michael-at-Bowes in Palmerston Road, designed by Sir George Gilbert Scott in Gothic Revival style and consecrated on 21 April 1874, six months before the new parish was constituted. The original church was demolished in 1986 and a new building consecrated on 7 June 1988.

The mission church of St Peter on the southeast corner of Brownlow Road and Bounds Green Road, was built in 1883; it was later replaced by

66. The Rev. John Thomas, the first Vicar of St Michael's, Wood Green.

67. St Michael's Church c.1906. It shows the church as completed in 1874, viewed from the south-west.

St Gabriel's, on the corner of Bounds Green Road and Durnsford Road, consecrated on 10 May 1906, while the original church became its parish hall and was eventually demolished in the 1930s to make way for a shopping precinct. The church prospered and a new hall adjacent to St Gabriel's was opened in 1937, but from the 1970s dwindling congregations and economies ultimately forced its closure in 1982 and dual use was made of the church hall; the church was demolished in 1983 and the hall a few years later. In 1982 the parish came under the St Michael's team ministry and the site of St Gabriel's has since been redeveloped, partly for housing, but a new church has yet to be built.

St Mark's, Noel Park, designed by Roland Plumbe, was consecrated in 1889; the adjacent church hall was built a few years earlier. In 1903, St Mark's had the highest Sunday attendance of all the Anglican churches in Wood Green.

St John's Mission Church in Brook Road was dedicated on 25 April 1898 in an area considered in particular need of salvation. Day-to-day running of the mission was taken over by the Church Army in 1929 and during the last war services were shared with the Salvation Army whose Citadel in nearby Mayes Road had been bombed. The mission building remains today but is in commercial use.

To the west the district chapelry of St Saviour, Alexandra Park Road, was created. A corrugated iron-clad church was dedicated on 11 January 1900 and replaced by a permanent building, designed by J.S. Alder, in February 1909. This was closed in 1993, demolished and replaced by a private housing development in 1998, but the war memorial erected in 1919 remains a permanent feature of the new estate.

St Andrew's, another iron church erected in 1900 on the corner of Alexandra Park Road and Windermere Road, just inside the Wood Green boundary, began as a mission church in 1899 meeting in the Norwegian House, a wooden building previously a restaurant in Alexandra Park. A new parish was created for it in March 1901 and a permanent church in red-brick,

68. *St Michael-at-Bowes, Palmerston Road in 1900, viewed from the south-west. It was demolished in 1986 to make way for a new building. The New River is in the foreground.*

designed by J.S. Alder to seat 800, was consecrated on 31 October 1903. St Andrew's was Alder's own parish church where he was sometime a sidesman. By the time of his death in 1919 he had built ten churches, 25 church halls and nine vicarages in the London area, several of them in Wood Green and neighbouring areas. Organisations attached to the church included a long running Literary Society, Orchestra and Drama Guild. The building was severely damaged by bombing on 19 February 1944 leaving only the walls standing. The parish hall became the temporary church until a new church, built using the old walls, was rededicated on 13 November 1957.

At the turn of the century another mission church was established in 1902 by the London Diocesan Home Mission in Wolves Lane for the Chitts Hill district. Again, it was an iron church which was replaced by a permanent building, again designed by J.S. Alder, dedicated to St Cuthbert, and consecrated in 1907.

The last mission to be established was the Church of the Good Shepherd in Stirling Road, to serve the 'Scotch Estate' on the east of the parish. Starting as an iron church in 1916 it was replaced by a new building in 1961.

69. *On the left is St Peter's Church, Brownlow Road, in 1914, which became the parish hall of St Gabriel's opposite.*

Since 1982, as a result of declining congregations, the services at St Gabriel's, St Michael-at-Bowes and The Good Shepherd have been conducted by a team ministry based on the parent church of St Michael. The Good Shepherd was closed early in 2000.

70. *St Saviour's Church, Alexandra Park Road, 1994. View from the north just before demolition, showing the war memorial.*

71. *St Andrew's Church, Alexandra Park Road c.1910. It shows the original iron church on the left.*

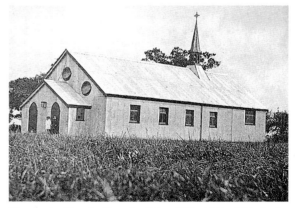

72. *St Cuthbert's Church, Chitts Hill, 1902. This is the original mission church which was replaced by the present building in 1907.*

73. The Baptist Church in Braemar Avenue, c.1910. The minister, Rev. W. Winston Haynes, is on the left.

PROTESTANT DISSENT

Quaker meetings were held in Tottenham at the end of the 17th century, but they never had a permanent meeting place in Wood Green, although they did use the Bradley Hall in Bradley Road between 1904-22.

Baptists were established in Tottenham High Road by 1830 and in rented rooms in Wood Green from 1837. The Wood Green Baptist Church itself was founded in 1865 in private rooms until the Baptist Chapel in Finsbury Road, seating 200, was built in 1875. This congregation maintained a mission in Station Road from 1886. A new church at the corner of Braemar Avenue seating 500, designed by George Baines, was opened in 1907. It later became the Braemar Avenue Baptist Church. The Bowes Park Baptist Church, a breakaway from the Wood Green church, registered its chapel in Palace Road in 1907 but reunited with Wood Green in 1914.

The story of the Westbury Avenue Baptist Church, at the corner of Wesbury Avenue and Willingdon Road, is interesting. This congregation began meeting in 1891 in a private house at no. 114 Turnpike Lane and a year later was known as Hornsey Park Baptist Church. On 11 August 1895 it held its first meeting at 'Dovecote Hall', a wooden shed in the grounds of no. 9 Dovecote Villas (later 78 High Road) which, since 1886, had been the home of a Strict Baptist congregation that had relocated to nearby Park Ridings in 1892. In 1902 the triangular plot of land formed by the junction of Westbury Avenue and Willingdon Road was offered by the developers to St Mark's Church, Noel Park, who built a corrugated iron mission hall on the site. The mission was unsuccessful and the hall was offered to the Congregationalists, but the Baptist pastor appealed for the hall for his flock. This was agreed by all parties and the 'tin tabernacle' opened for Baptist worship on 21 September 1902, and was registered under the name of Westbury Avenue Church (Baptist). By 1920 the congregation had grown to over 200, swollen by the extension of the Noel Park Estate. The existing red-brick building in Westbury Avenue, seating 300, was dedicated on 24 May 1930.

The Strict Baptists mentioned above in Park Ridings replaced their chapel with a red-brick building in 1923 known as Wood Green Strict Baptist Chapel, but a section of the congregation moved back to Dovecote Hall in 1909 until 1911 when they established an iron church in Eldon Road which was rebuilt in 1936, known as Dovecote Baptist Chapel, along with a church hall.

CONGREGATIONALISTS

Congregationalists began holding meetings in the area from 1861 and built the first non-conformist church in Wood Green a few years later. Their Wood Green Congregational Chapel in Lordship Lane was opened on 5 January 1864, seating 500; it was designed by Lander and Bedell and built by local builder Edward Clarke of West Green at a cost of just under £2000. A Sunday School was added to the rear in Redvers Road in 1887. The chapel functioned until 1964 when the congregation joined with the Harringay Congregational Church which had been established in Green Lanes in 1902. The Lordship Lane building was then acquired by the local authority and functioned for some years as the Haringey Arts Centre before being leased for commercial purposes. Its future became uncertain because of redevelopment plans in 1998 but as a result of local campaigning it is likely to be retained for community use.

The Bowes Park Congregational Church began in 1902 with a hall and schoolrooms at the corner of Arcadian Gardens and the High Road. The adjacent large red-brick church was registered in 1912. The congregation joined with that of St James Presbyterian Church in 1950, and later became the United Reformed Church of St James-at-Bowes. Since the 1980s the building has served the congregation of the New Testament of God. The Alexandra Park Congregational Church in Alexandra Park Road was registered in 1907.

74. *The Congregational Chapel in Lordship Lane, c.1905. Opened in 1864, it became the Haringey Arts Centre in 1965, and is now in commercial use.*

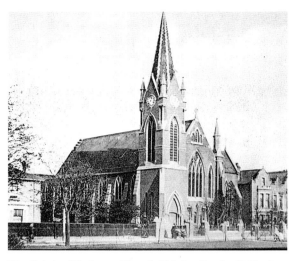

75. *Trinity Wesleyan Chapel, Trinity Road c.1910. It became the Greek Orthodox Cathedral of St Mary in 1970.*

METHODISTS

Wesleyan Methodists held open-air meetings on waste land that was to become Trinity Gardens from 1864. On 20 April 1871 the foundation stone of Trinity Chapel was laid by Sir Francis Lycett MP and it was dedicated in 1872. This was the first chapel erected with the aid of a fund provided by Sir Francis to build fifty Wesleyan chapels in London and its suburbs. In 1903 it had the highest Sunday attendances of all the non-conformist churches in the area. The Wesleyan Methodists also established a church seating 1000 in Palmerston Road.

Primitive Methodists met in a private house in Finsbury Road in 1882. They opened a chapel on the north side of Station Road in 1882 and relocated to the south side of the road in 1908. This chapel was closed in 1939 and disappeared in the redevelopments of the 1960s.

Welsh Calvinistic Methodists established an iron chapel on the corner of Northcott Avenue and Bounds Green Road in 1906. They moved to the former Baptist Chapel in Palace Road in 1915.

PRESBYTERIANS

The Presbyterian Church of England came to Wood Green in 1875, occupying an iron church previously used by the Church of Scotland. By 1879, St James's Presbyterian Church, a solid and ornate red-brick building, had been built at the corner of the High Road and Canning Crescent.

In 1903 morning and evening attendances reached around 500, among the highest Presbyterian figures in London at that time. In 1950 the congregation combined with the Bowes Park Congregational Church and St James's was used as a warehouse before demolition in the late 1970s. The site is now occupied by flats.

In 1903, the total attendance at the many nonconformist churches in Wood Green was double that of the Anglican churches.

ROMAN CATHOLICS

A Roman Catholic revival in Tottenham began in the 1790s, but a Roman Catholic parish of St Paul, Wood Green, was not created until 1882. Its first church, an iron building in Station Road, was erected that year, and by 1903 Sunday attendances reached 822. A larger brick church in Romanesque style, designed by E. Goldie, was built alongside the original building in 1904, the latter becoming a church hall. These were replaced in 1970 when a new building, designed by John Rochford was opened. Stained glass from the second church features in the corridor of the present church.

76. St James's Presbyterian Church c.1905. It stood on the corner of High Road and Canning Crescent and was demolished c.1970.

77. St Paul's Roman Catholic Church, Station Road, c.1905. Its original iron church is to the right.

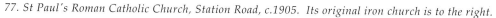

78. The opening of the Salvation Army Citadel in Mayes Road in 1890., From a wood block print.

OTHER DENOMINATIONS

The Salvation Army had a barracks in Finsbury Road between 1884-96 and the Wood Green Citadel, on the corner of Mayes Road and Alexandra Road, was opened with much pomp and circumstance in 1890. It was seriously damaged during the last war but after repair it remained until the mid-1970s when demolished to make way for the building of Shopping City. A new meeting place, the Salvation Army Wood Green Christian Centre, was opened in Lymington Avenue in 1976.

Wood Green attracted a number of smaller sects who had not previously been seen in Tottenham. A group known as Christian Brethren had mission rooms in Station Road between 1885 and 1960 and met at the Ringslade Hall in Ringslade Road in 1928. Unitariarians were established in Wood Green by 1890 and Unity Hall in Newnham Road was opened in 1894 (rebuilt in 1902). It was closed in 1966 and later demolished to make way for redevelopment.

The Catholic Apostolic Church occupied the former Baptist Chapel in Finsbury Road in 1906

79. The Salvation Army Citadel in Mayes Road c.1910.

until 1965 and in the 1930s the Church of the Truth Seeker occupied the former Methodist chapel in Northcott Avenue.

Several Spiritualist groups were based in Wood Green. One met in the Bradley Hall in 1926-32 and in Stuart House, River Park Road from 1932-54. The Temple of the Trinity of Spiritual Healing met at no. 371 High Road between 1937-41. The

Sanctuary of St Andrew held meetings at No.65 Duckett Road from 1942-65. The Wood Green Spiritualist Church has met in a private house in Maryland Road since 1953.

The Elim Foursquare Gospel Alliance met in the Brook Hall, Brook Road between 1930-55. Jehovah Witnesses were at nos. 6-8 Westbury Avenue from 1938-53 and in the Adult School in Commerce Road from 1962-72 before moving to Bowes Road.

After the last war traditional congregations declined leading to mergers and amalgamations. By contrast, and as a result of West Indian immigration from the 1950s, new evangelical congregations were established, some of them taking over redundant chapels and churches. The former Calvinistic Methodist Chapel in Northcott Avenue became the Wood Green Seventh Day Adventist Church by 1952 and a new building was erected in 1972. The Mayes Road Mission Hall (now demolished), on the corner of Hornsey Park Road became the Wood Green Evangelical Church by 1957 which moved to the former Baptist Chapel in Park Ridings in 1971; the chapel now houses a Grace Baptist church. The former United Reformed Church on the corner of Arcadian Gardens and the High Road is now a New Testament Church of God.

Immigration from Cyprus began in the mid-fifties with Cypriots settling in the north of Wood Green and Palmers Green and in the Green Lanes area of Harringay. In 1965 the Greek Orthodox Church took over the former Baptist Chapel in Finsbury Road to establish the St Barnabas Community. In 1970 they acquired the nearby former Trinity Chapel, in Trinity Road, which became the Greek Orthodox Cathedral of St Mary. Despite a serious fire in 1980, leaving only the walls and spire, the church was rebuilt in sympathy with its predecessor, and today remains a focus for the north London Greek community.

At the present time planning applications have been submitted for the use of two of Wood Green's landmark buildings, the former Congregational Chapel in Lordship Lane and the former Gaumont Palace Cinema, by evangelical religous groups.

80. The former Baptist Church in Finsbury Road c.1910, which today is St Barnabas Greek Orthodox Church.

SYNAGOGUES AND MOSQUES

Athough a strong Jewish community was established in Tottenham by the turn of the 20th century, it was small in Wood Green and no synagogues were built within its boundaries. However, two synagogues were located close to its northern and southern borders. The Hornsey and Wood Green Synagogue was founded in 1920 in a temporary building in Wightman Road (Hornsey) until a new synagogue, seating 200, was built on the same site and opened in 1959. By 1976 it had become part of the United Synagogue based at Upper Woburn Place, but was subsequently closed. Post-war, a small Jewish community became concentrated in Woodfield Way, Bounds Green which used the Palmers Green Synagogue in Brownlow Road.

An example of cultural diversity in recent years is the use of the former Hornsey and Wood Green Synagogue in Wightman Road as an Islamic mosque and cultural centre in 1988-89. The site is designated for Haringey's first purpose-built mosque.

QUEEN'S COLLEGE,

WOOD GREEN,

Will Re-open on the 12th of September next,

HOURS OF ATTENDANCE FOR DAY PUPILS

DURING THE MICHAELMAS TERM:—

From 10 a.m. to 1 p.m., and

„ 2.30 to 4.30 p.m.

THE

WOOD GREEN LADIES' COLLEGE,

HAVELOCK HOUSE,

PELLATT'S GROVE, WOOD GREEN,

LONDON, N.

Principals:—

MRS. AND MISS BAKER.

Head English Master:—

H. DEXTER, Esq.

Visiting Professors—

(ALSO TWO RESIDENT GOVERNESSES).

MRS. AND MISS BAKER continue to receive a limited number of Young Ladies as Resident Pupils, to impart to them a First-class and Finished Education.

This Establishment offers superior advantages to those Parents who are anxious to obtain for their Children a happy Christian Home, combined with the judicious arrangements of a refined and well-regulated College. The mind here is educated, not the memory taught; the disposition carefully and judiciously trained; the character formed, and refinement of manners cultivated. They are liberally boarded at the same table with the Principals; affectionately treated, and their health watched over with anxious solicitude.

The mode of tuition is adapted to each, separately as well as collectively, to both Senior and Junior Students, thereby contributing to the happiness of the Pupils, as well as securing rapid improvement.

The course of Instruction is comprehensive, including English in all its branches, Writing, Arithmetic, French, Music, Singing, Drawing, Dancing, with Calisthenics, German, Italian, and Latin.

Terms, very moderate (either inclusive or distinct), may be had with Prospectus of the College, on application to the Principals.

References kindly permitted to the Parents of present and former Pupils.

The next Session will commence, D.V., on the 18th of July, 1870.

EDUCATION AND HAPPY HOME FOR YOUNG LADIES.

Inclusive terms, with or without vacation, £6 and £7 per quarter, commencing day of entrance.

Mrs. DUNBAR and Miss E. COOMBES,

ALEXANDRA HOUSE, GREEN LANES, WOOD GREEN.

THE

Rev. M. S. BROMET,

RESIDING AT

"DURLEY VILLA," BROOK ROAD,

WOOD GREEN,

Begs to inform the Public of this neigh=bourhood that he intends forming

FRENCH CLASSES

FOR YOUNG GENTLEMEN AND OTHERS.

TERMS:

1s. per Lesson; or £1 1s. per Quarter, Twice a Week.

PRIVATE LESSONS—Two Guineas per Quarter.

SCHOOLS undertaken for 10s. 6d. per Quarter for each Pupil.

Three Lessons per week.

CONVERSATIONAL CLASSES FOR MORE ADVANCED PUPILS.

ST. JOHN'S COLLEGE,

WOOD GREEN, TOTTENHAM.

Principal—J. B. BAKER, M.R.C.P.,

Assisted by Four Resident English and Foreign Masters.

Terms:

Including a sound English, French, Latin, Greek, and Mathematical Education, with German, Music, Drawing, Book-keeping, Shorthand, Chemistry, Engineering, Natural Philosophy, Drilling, Land Surveying, Board, Laundress, all Books, and Extras of every kind,

26, 28 and 30 GUINEAS per ANNUM,

According to Age.

DAY PUPILS' INCLUSIVE TERMS—

Under 8 Years of Age	- - - - -	1 Guinea
Do. 11 do.	- - - - -	1½ „
Above 11 do.	- - - - -	2 Guineas

per Quarter.

Pianoforte Instruction (if required) Half a Guinea per Quarter; Drilling 1s. 6d. per Quarter.

The above Terms include Copy, Exercise, and Ciphering Books, Pens, Ink, and Preparation for any Business, Profession, or Examination.

There are no extra charges of any kind, except Printed Books and Drawing Materials, which Parents have the option of purchasing themselves.

The House and Grounds are extensive and beautifully situated. Inspection of the Domestic arrangements solicited. Special attention is paid to Mercantile Education. Testimonials, with References, of the highest order. Parents who are seeking for a thorough Educational Establishment, where the Pupils are most kindly treated, liberally boarded, carefully trained, and by a judicious course of studies, rapidly prepared for any examination, profession, or business, are respectfully solicited to apply to the Principal.

---

81. *Advertisements for local private schools in the Northern Advertiser, August 1870.*

Places of Learning

Although the provision of schools within the parish of Tottenham extended back three centuries or so there were none in the Wood Green Ward until the 19th century. The emerging middle class population of Wood Green probably sent their children to the established Tottenham schools or to other local private schools or, especially in the case of girls, educated them at home. There were private schools in Tottenham as early as 1670 and several Quaker boarding schools there during the 18th and early 19th centuries.

PRIVATE SCHOOLS

Wood Green had three private schools in 1839, six by 1862, eleven in 1870, fourteen in 1874 and eighteen in 1878. They were variously described as 'ladies' school', 'grammar school', 'ladies' college', 'preparatory school', 'boarding school' etc. and were in private houses often with only one or two teachers. Their advertisements make interesting reading. Many of them were short-lived and their educational achievements unrecorded, but others survived for up to two decades or more until the demand for this type of schooling declined in the 1890s. One of the later arrivals in Wood Green was the renowned Clark's College, founded in Southgate Road, Stoke Newington, in 1880, and which opened a branch at 'The Hollies' in Stuart Crescent in 1909. It offered general and commercial education for over 100 pupils in 1949, but its operations ceased at Wood Green in 1960.

Another landmark school was the Royal Masonic Institution's Boys' School in Lordship Lane. This was founded in 1857 for the sons of deceased and needy freemasons, in the former Lordship Lodge, on an estate of 10 acres. Originally catering for 70 boys, the old house was replaced by a substantial Gothic building, designed by Edwin Pearce and J.B. Wilson and Son in 1865, with accomodation for 200 boys. According to Thorne (1876) the school provided a thorough commercial education. It moved to Bushey, Hertfordshire in 1898 after Princess Alexandra had presented prizes at the final prize-giving in Wood Green.

The site was then sold to the Home and Colonial School Society, founded in 1836, which opened its Training College for Schoolmistresses in 1904. The training college remained for almost three decades but in 1930 the site was sold to the Tottenham District Gas Co., and the building renamed Woodall House, after its chairman, Sir Colbert Woodall. It later became the offices of

82. *The original Royal Masonic Institution's Boys' School, Lordship Lane c.1860. It was previously a private residence.*

83. *Classroom scene in the Royal Masonic Institution's Boys' School, c.1880.*

84. *The Home & Colonial School Society Training College in Lordship Lane, formerly the Royal Masonic Institute for Boys, was opened by the Archbishop of Canterbury on 27 January 1904. A dedication service was held at the chapel, at which the Bishop of Islington preached. A reception was held afterwards in the large assembly hall. This picture includes a number of civic dignitaries, under the chairmanship of the Dean of Peterborough.*

85. *A gymnasium class at the Home & Colonial Training College, c.1920.*

Eastern Gas until the site was acquired by Haringey Council in 1974. The building was modernised and became the Wood Green Crown Court, opened in 1989, and the rest of the site developed for housing.

CHURCH SCHOOLS

The provision of public education before state intervention in 1870 fell largely to the churches who from 1811 acted in collaboration with the National Society for the Education of the Poor in the Principles of the Established Church – hence the so-called 'National' schools. Wood Green's first elementary school, St Michael's National Day School, opened in 1859 in the Sunday School building adjacent to the Church. This building was enlarged in 1863 and confined to infants after a new senior school was built in 1872 on the opposite side of Bounds Green Road. The latter was built by public subscription, the site being the gift of Mrs Pearson of Nightingale Hall. Designed for 300 boys and girls it had 420 pupils in 1898. The infants' school was further enlarged in 1886 and remained in use until the opening of a new junior school, built on the site of the senior school between 1966 and 1972, when it was formally opened by the Duke of Gloucester.

86. *Providence Convent High School in Stuart Crescent.*

A Roman Catholic infants and junior school was established by St Paul's Church, Station Road, in 1884, occupying a new building in Bradley Road from 1885. This was rebuilt in the late 1960s. A second Catholic primary school, St Martin of Porres, opened in Blake Road in 1972. The Providence Convent School for girls was established by the Daughters of Providence at the request of St Paul's Church in 1905. It first occupied no.10 Broseley Villas in Bounds Green Road, which had previously been a ladies' college. No. 9 Broseley Villas was acquired the next year and by 1907 numbers had reached 200 and the school moved to nos. 19-20 Stuart Crescent,

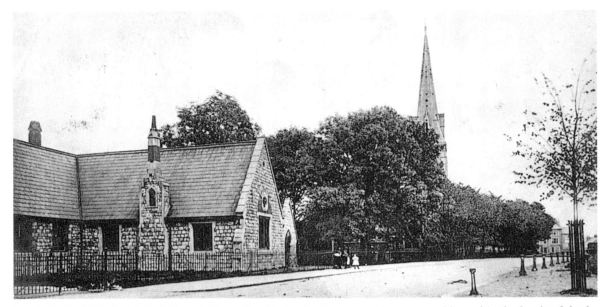

87. *St Michael's Infant School, Bounds Green Road in 1903. It was opened in 1859 and housed in the Sunday School building adjacent to the church.*

the former home of a private school called Queen's College. In subsequent expansion it acquired no. 18 Stuart Crescent and Brabançonne Villa in the High Road in 1921, the latter serving as the senior school while the juniors remained at Stuart Crescent. The whole school was relocated to a new building in Earlham Grove in the grounds of Brabançonne Villa, opened in 1926 as St Angela's Providence Convent High School. Unable to meet comprehensive requirements on the Earlham Grove site the school transferred to a new St Angela's R.C. School for Girls in Oakthorpe Road, Palmers Green, in 1975. The former school building in Earlham Grove now functions as the Cypriot Community Centre.

BOARD SCHOOLS

The 1870 Education Act was introduced to overcome the inability of the churches and chapels to keep pace with the education of a growing population. It provided for the establishment of local boards in charge of providing schools and eduction for infants and juniors. The Tottenham School Board was set up in 1879 and retained responsibility for Wood Green until 1903.

Wood Green's first elementary board school was inaugurated in 1880 with boys meeting in Congregational Church premises in Lordship

Lane, girls in the Baptist Chapel in Finsbury Road and infants in a Temperance hall. It was brought together under one roof in the new White Hart Lane School in 1884. This was followed by others at Bounds Green (1888), meeting in temporary accommodation until the school on the corner of Bounds Green and Park Roads was opened in 1895, Noel Park (1889) and the Alexandra Board School in Western Road (1894) accommodated in an iron building until it was replaced with new buildings in 1901. A temporary Board School was opened in Gladstone Avenue in 1889 and was transferred to a new building in Lordship Lane in 1906. All these schools were built in the red brick of the time. The White Hart Lane elementary school survived until 1939 when its younger pupils were amalgamated into the nearby Earlham Grove junior and infant schools, renamed Earlham School in 1968. Their old building was used as an adult education centre in the post-war years and was eventually demolished in the 1980s to make way for housing. The Bounds Green, Alexandra, Lordship Lane and Noel Park buildings remain in use today as primary schools.

Higher Grade Board schools provided secondary education for pupils of 11+ who were not selected for grammar schools. The Wood Green Higher Grade school was in fact the first option to Tottenham Grammar School for local chil-

88. *Bounds Green Board Schools, c.1910.*

89. *Higher Grade School, Bounds Green Road, c.1904. This building, opened in 1899, subsequently housed Central, Grammar and Comprehensives and is now a Primary school.*

90. Lordship Lane Elementary Board School, c.1912.

dren. It was set up in 1884 using rented premises: boys were at the Wesleyan Chapel in Trinity Road and girls at the Presbyterian Church Sunday School in Canning Crescent. A new building in Bounds Green Road opened in 1899, as the Wood Green Higher Grade School. In 1918, it became Wood Green Central School.

Under the Balfour Education Act (1902) the expenses of elementary education fell to the local authority. The Wood Green Education Committee, established in 1903, created new schools at Lordship Lane (1906), the temporary Muswell Hill School in Albert Road (1908) which closed in 1920, Rhodes Avenue infants and juniors (1930), Earlham Grove (1939) which took infants and juniors from White Hart Lane and a separate infants' school at Rhodes Avenue (1952).

GRAMMAR SCHOOLS

In 1921 responsibility for secondary education passed to the Middlesex County Council and the former Higher Grade School underwent several changes in name to become the mixed Trinity County School in 1924 and the largest secondary school in Middlesex. In 1944 it became Trinity County Grammar School.

The MCC had already established Wood Green's first mixed grammar school in 1910, the Wood Green County School, with its command-ing position in Glendale Avenue overlooking Woodside Park. It later became known as Glendale County Grammar School.

In 1962 the two County grammar schools, Glendale and Trinity, were amalgamated to become Wood Green County Grammar School, and transferred to new buildings in White Hart Lane.

SECONDARY MODERNS TO COMPREHENSIVES

The 1944 Education Act brought in secondary education for every child nationwide and the transfer of control to the county councils. Secondary modern schools were set up at Cecil Rhodes in Rhodes Avenue in 1959 (mixed), Woodside (boys) in Glendale Avenue from 1962, with Parkwood (girls) occupying the former Trinity County School building in Bounds Green Road from 1963.

The introduction of comprehensive education in 1967 also saw the creation of Alexandra Park with its lower school in Park Road and an upper school at the former Cecil Rhodes in 1975. The Wood Green Comprehensive School incorporated boys from Wood Green County Grammar and Woodside and girls from Parkwood; the upper school at White Hart Lane and the lower at Glendale Avenue.

91. St Thomas More R.C. School, Glendale Avenue, 1995. It was built in 1910 as Wood Green County School.

St Thomas More Roman Catholic School for boys originated as a secondary modern school in Holcombe Road, Tottenham, in 1952. It became a comprehensive school in 1968 with the upper school located at the former Trinity County School in Bounds Green Road. The whole school was eventually rehoused in the former Glendale school building in Glendale Avenue where it is today.

The former Higher Grade School building in Bounds Green Road survives today, unchanged externally, as the Nightingale Primary School.

FURTHER EDUCATION

The Workers' Education Association ran adult courses in Wood Green from 1910 and an Adult School was established about the same time in premises in Commerce Road and Brook Road.

92. Rhodes Avenue New School, opened October 1930.

Retiring Places

From the 16th century benefactors in the parish of Tottenham paid for the building of almshouses for the poor and needy. Typical of these were the Pound's (pre-1600), Sanchez' (1600) and Reynardson's (1737) almshouses in the area of of Tottenham High Road.

But from the middle of the 19th century Wood Green became a favoured location for almshouses established by City institutions, which welcomed the cheaper sites and the cleaner and quieter environment.

FISHMONGERS AND POULTERERS

The foundation stone of the Fishmongers' and Poulterers' Almshouses was laid by Lord Morpeth on 25 June 1847 on the west of the High Road just north of St Michael's Church. A fund-raising notice at the time hoped that:

> others blessed with the means of alleviating the accumulated misery of sickness and poverty (the attendants upon old age) brought frequently to premature decay by constant exposure to wet and weather in catering for the pleasures of their wealthier fellow-citizens, may see sufficient reason to induce their kind support and generous aid on the present occasion.

The building, designed by Mee and William Webb in Tudor style with a central turreted gateway, for 12 married couples, was opened in 1849. Generosity was not immediate and twelve years later two of the houses remained unoccupied due to lack of funds. Nevertheless, the almshouses survived as a well-known landmark until 1955 when they were demolished to make way for the building of the Wood Green (later Haringey) Civic Centre.

PRINTERS' ALMSHOUSES

The Printers' Pension Society Asylum (commonly known as The Printers' Almshouses), inaugurated by Lord Stanhope in June 1856, was on the south side of Bounds Green Road opposite St Michael's church. The building, also designed by William Webb in Tudor style, consisted of three ranges around a courtyard facing the road. Originally, it housed 12 couples, each occupying a sitting room, bedroom and kitchen, who received a weekly allowance. It was enlarged with extra wings in 1871 to accommodate 24 couples and further extended in 1891. It was closed in 1969 and demolished in 1970 to make way for a telecoms switching centre.

93. The Fishmongers' & Poulterers' Almshouses in c.1905. It was later the site of the Wood Green Civic Centre in 1956.

94. *The Printers' Almshouses in 1858. View from the High Road, looking towards Bounds Green Road. St Michael's chapel-of-ease is on the right and Georgian cottages are in the distance.*

95. *The Duchess of Albany opening an extension to the Printers' Almshouses. Pictorial World, 24 October 1891.*

UNITED CHARITIES OF ST LEONARD SHOREDITCH ALMSHOUSES

Judge John Fuller's Almshouses were originally built in Old Street, Shoreditch *c*. 1605 and rebuilt in 1787. Their site was required to build a town hall and fire station and as a result new almshouses in Gothic style, designed by C.A. Long, were erected in Nightingale Road, Wood Green in 1866. Fuller's Almshouses were later incorporated into the United Charities of St Leonard, Shoreditch a body which in 1904 re-built them for 12 women and also St Leonard's House for four married couples and the Porter's and Walter's Almshouses for 16 women, all designed by Alfred Cross on the same site. These buildings, now listed Grade II, remain today. Recently, new accomodation provided by the United Charities has been erected in adjacent Truro Road.

96. Memorial stone at the time of the demolition of the Printers' Almshouses c.1970. The site is now a telecom centre.

97. St Leonard's House and Porters' and Walters Almshouses, Nightingale Road, soon after completion in 1904.

A Little Industry

Wood Green grew as a residential area and later became an important north London shopping centre. However, some of its few manufacturing industries also helped to put it on the map and date from early times. These sites tended to be at the extremities of the district.

CLAY TILES AND POTS

The first industrial activity in the area took advantage of an indigenous product, the rich deposits of London clay. Brick-making had been established in Tottenham and surrounding parishes since the 15th century. The first clay workings in the Wood Green area were located at the southernmost extremity of the Wood Green ward alongside Beans Green, on a site which later became the Harringay Stadium and Arena, and now is home for a Sainsbury's Superstore. These clay workings and their associated tile kilns were well established by 1798 when they were owned by Nathaniel V. Lee; by 1843 thirteen cottages had been built for the workers. These works became Williamson's Potteries in the later part of the 19th century and closed in the early 1900s, the workers' cottages being condemned on health grounds in 1905.

Clay pits with tile kilns and potteries were established at Bounds Green by 1862 by Charles

98. Samuel South (1853-1919), son of the founder of South's pottery.

99. Clay digging at South's pottery in White Hart Lane, shortly before closure in 1960.

100. Potmaker hand-throwing garden pots c.1960.

Paul Millard, then described as 'brick and tile maker'; he was mentioned earlier as a property developer. By 1903 the Bounds Green Pottery was owned by Charles Pickering and specialised in glazed bricks and tiles. Operations ceased by 1926 when the site was sold to the Wood Green District Scouts and in 1928 renamed Scout Park which it remains today. Some of the original buildings remain and the levels of the workings can still be seen.

Two potteries also existed on the north side of White Hart Lane close to Devonshire Hill, formerly known as Clay Hill, perhaps indicating earlier brick-working in the area. Their location was described as 'Apeland' in the 1619 Survey. By the mid-19th century the land, then part of Tent Farm, had been leased in two parts as 'brickground' to Samuel Johnson and 'potteries' to Edward Cole. The Cole family claim their business was established elsewhere in 1805. Cole's pottery in White Hart Lane, known as the Tottenham Potteries, existed from 1856 to the mid-1950s. This site later became a Williams Brothers Direct Supply Stores Depot.

The neighbouring potter, Johnson, sold his interest to the Nottinghamshire pot maker, Richard Sankey who was unable to compete with Cole and left. Meanwhile, Joseph South, who came from Barley, Hertfordshire, set up a pottery in Dysons Road, Edmonton in 1868 to produce flower pots for the expanding Lea Valley market garden industry. In 1874 Joseph South sold the Dysons Road pottery to his son, Samuel, before emigrating.

The young Samuel South acquired the Sankey operation in 1886 and transferred his business to White Hart Lane where it became known as

101. The third generation Samuel South (1909-1968) with the smallest and largest pots.

the White Hart Lane Potteries. The business became one of the largest horticultural potmakers in Britain, producing up to 100,000 hand-made pots a week. It used traditional hand-forming techniques, employing at peak times 150 men. Up to 100 horses were also used at the works and provided an important secondary business in general cartage and refuse collection. During the First World War the horses were requisitioned for active service. Samuel South died in 1919 the business passing to his son, also Samuel, who died in 1956 when the business passed to his two elder sons. It was, however, unable to compete with the larger firms, or with mechanisation and the introduction of plastic pots, and clay pot making in Wood Green ceased on 5 October 1960 when the business was sold to the soft drinks company, Idris Ltd, for development. The site was subsequently used for light industry and for a time was occupied by Beechams. Examples of South's pots and other artefacts are held in the Bruce Castle Museum.

The proximity of the two potteries in White Hart Lane enouraged friendly rivalry. In 1936 a local newspaper attempted to compare the aggregate length of service of their respective employees. Analysis showed that for the longest serving 21 employees, at Cole's they totalled 891 years against South's 885 years; an average of 42.5 years for each of the Cole's workers!

TOBACCO AND PIANOFORTES
South of Wood Green Common between Mayes Road, Hornsey Park Road and the GNR railway line was a site, depicted on the 1864 OS map, of a 'tobacco manufactory'. This was the tobacco, snuff and cigar factory of Edward Welch, established by 1861 at the end of Western Road, with the proprietor's house and workers' cottages adjacent. By 1894 the factory had gone and the site had become part of the Hornsey Gas Works, with its two distinctive gas holders which remain today.

By 1872 a Henry Ivory had established Allsopp & Co.'s pianoforte factory in the Mayes Road area. This was to play an important part in the future development of the immediate area.

CHOCOLATES AND SWEETS
In 1848 George Osborne Barratt founded a sweet factory in Shepherdess Walk, Islington. Needing to expand his business he acquired the Allsopp piano factory and transferred there in 1880. Thus began the rapid expansion of Barratt & Co., Confectionery Manufacturers, on a site bounded by Mayes Road, Western Road and Coburg Road. They acquired the site of Woodlands. a large house at the corner of Mayes Road, and built their distinctive single-storey building, originally the stables for their cart-horses, which faced Wood Green Common for almost one hundred years. Their imposing office block in Mayes Road was completed in 1897. Other buildings were added in 1914, 1922, 1936 and 1953. Barratt's progressed from a small family business to a large public company but remained a benevolent employer who provided at its peak nearly 1000 jobs and some housing for local people. Their products, including Caxton Chocolate, Liquorice Allsorts, Gold Flake Sweet Varieties etc. will be remembered with affection as will the related odours that pervaded the atmosphere of this part of Wood Green during their manufacture. In the 1950s about 1,000 tons of Barratt's sweets were exported annually worldwide. The company was acquired in 1966 by the Bassett (later Trebor-Bassett) Group and in 1980 when sweet manufacturing in Wood Green ceased.

The verbose commentator on the North London suburbs, Thomas Burke, generally disparaging about Wood Green, waxed lyrical over

102. George Osborne Barratt (1827-1906).

Barratt's in the 1920s with the words:

> Barratt & Co. are to Wood Green what Shakespeare is to Stratford, Johnson to Litchfield, Mrs Gaskell to Knutsford, Coleridge to Highgate.

Furthermore, he was moved to verse:

> I think I will go to Wood Green
> Where the toffee-apples grow,
> And in the darkling green wood
> See the pear-drops glow.
> I will build a house of almond-rock,
> And fence it all around
> With stout sticks of barley sugar
> Planted in the ground.
>
> I will bore for a spring of mineral water
> Warranted to contain
> No "deleterious matter"
> To bring a morning pain.
> I will have a floor of chocolate bars
> and a settee of Turkish delight;
> and Barratt shall put me to bed an night,
> and Co. shall wait on me.

The Barratt site had a new lease of life during

103. Barratt's office building in Mayes Road, c.1905. It is now occupied by the Metropolitan Housing Trust.

104. Barratt's factory facing Wood Green Common c.1928. It is now replaced by a social services office.

the 1980s as part of the Wood Green Industrial Area with new businesses making use of the old buildings and erecting new ones for light industrial use. In the 1990s part of the area was redesignated as The Business Centre of Wood Green.. More recently, one of the former Barratt buildings became The Chocolate Factory, a centre for cultural and artistic enterprises.

In 1999 the whole area was planned for renewal as 'The Haringey Heartlands' (see p.139).

LIGHT INDUSTRY AND GARDENING

A number of light engineering concerns have been based in Wood Green. A glassworks was established at Bounds Green by 1910 on part of the former Bounds Green Farm, on the north side of Cline Road. This became the Standard Bottle Co. Ltd in 1921. It was destroyed by fire in the 1970s, but one of its larger buildings was subsequently taken by Middlesex Polytechnic and is now part of the Middlesex University Campus.

The scientific instrument makers, R.W. Munro, makers of the renowned air speed indicator adopted by meteorological offices world wide, were also located in Cline Road.

The Wonder Baking Co. set up its 'Wonderloaf' factory on the north side of White Hart Lane, next door to South's Potteries, in 1937.

Market gardening became big business in Edmonton, Enfield and Tottenham, along the more fertile banks of the Lea river, during the 18th and 19th centuries. Even in 1902 Tottenham

105. *The caramel and toffee room at Barratt's factory, c.1950.*

106. *Barratt's horse-drawn delivery vehicles.*

had eighteen nurseries and twenty florists. Many of the early larger Wood Green houses had kitchen gardens and probably sold surplus produce locally. According to Kelly's Directories the following nurseries were located in the Wood Green area: Wood Green Nursery, Commerce Road (1864); Bowes Nursery (James Pate) (1871); The Vineries (Wm. G. Hazell), Nightingale Road (1882-1884); Alexandra Nurseries (Maurice Ahern), Woodside Road (1903). In addition there were at least six jobbing nurserymen, probably servicing the larger houses, in the latter half of the 19th century. By the 1920s the Alexandra Nurseries site had become the Wood Green UDC Nursery accessed from Wolves Lane and is now Haringey Council's nursery known as Palm House. Bounds Green Nurseries stood on the north side of Bounds Green Road, from *c*.1910 to 1960, after which flats were built on the site.

LAUNDRIES

Laundries, one of the first service industries, quickly became established, finding particular favour with middle-class Wood Green residents. Most had their receiving offices in the local shopping streets with their works elsewhere. Two exceptions were the Wood Green & Hornsey Steam Laundry Ltd. in Albert Road, established in the 1890s, with its works alongside the Muswell Stream. Its buildings, with a distinctive boiler chimney, remain today in alternative use. The other, the Mirror Laundry, with its single-storey twin-gabled building, was located in Brabant Road from 1910 until at least the outbreak of the last war. It later became a community centre and survives today as a children's playcentre.

The largest local laundry, the MAP (Myddleton and Alexandra Park), opened around 1906 in The Campsbourne, Hornsey, resulted from a merger between the Myddleton Road (Bowes Park) and Alexandra Park Laundries. It once employed several hundred workers.

COWKEEPERS AND DAIRYMEN

In the 1860s and '70s the supply of fresh milk fell to local cowkeepers and dairymen who delived by hand- or pony-cart two or three times a day. By the 1890s larger dairy farms (see p.32) had retail shops in Wood Green. These larger operations were eventually taken over by national operations such as the Express Dairy and United Dairies by the 1920s, which also used milk brought in by train from wider afield. However, some of the one-man operations survived even to recent times: a cowkeeper was recorded in Redvers Road in 1934 and at least five dairymen were still in business in Wood Green in 1957.

Cowkeeper William South established his yard in Stuart Crescent in 1872, which was taken over by the Sexton Bros. Dairy by 1898.

107. Sexton's Dairy milk roundsmen in Truro Road in 1905. Their dairy yard was at no. 25 Stuart Crescent and survived until the 1920s.

For the BEST LAUNDRY WORK.

WOOD GREEN & HORNSEY LAUNDRY

OPEN-AIR DRYING.

We use 4 million gallons of water yearly.

Punctual Collection and Delivery.

Our Shirt and Collar Ironing and Shaping Appliances give an exceptionally beautiful finish to gentlemen's linen with the minimum of wear.

PRICE LISTS POST FREE.

The Wood Green and Hornsey Steam Laundry, Ltd.,

ALBERT ROAD, WOOD GREEN, N.

108. *Advertisement for the Wood Green and Hornsey Laundry. From the Wood Green Guide 1910.*

109. *The delivery van of the Myddleton Laundry c.1905, based in The Campsbourne, Hornsey.*

A Palace for the People

The story of Alexandra Palace and Park is integral to that of Wood Green. This Victorian enterprise has been the subject of many trials and tribulations, but it has, nevertheless, dominated Wood Green from its lofty position on the western boundary.

The first plans for a Palace of the People in the style of the Crystal Palace, on the site of the former Tottenham Wood Farm, were proposed by the designer Owen Jones in 1858 but did not materialise. In 1862 the North London Park & Land Co. put up proposals to develop the estate as park and housing, but this scheme went no further. In the following year the Alexandra Park Co. Ltd. acquired the farmland for conversion to a park and to build the People's Palace which had been proposed by Owen Jones. The park of 250 acres, was opened in 1863 and named after Princess Alexandra of Denmark who had married Edward, Prince of Wales (later Edward VII), earlier that year. A Tudor style banqueting hall, later called the Blandford Hall, was erected in 1864 and the horse racing course opened on 30 June 1868.

The first Palace was designed by Alfred Meeson and work started in 1864 using a substantial quantity of materials from the 1862 International Exhibition in Kensington. The Alexandra Park Co. ran into financial difficulties, a foretaste of things to come, and work was delayed. Two further companies came to the rescue to allow the building to open on 24 May 1873. Tragedy struck sixteen days later when the Palace was burnt to the ground.

The second Palace designed by John Johnson, a partner of Meeson, was opened on 1 May 1875 within just two years of the earlier disaster. The new building, occupying seven and a half acres, featured the Great Hall with seating for 14,000, a Willis Organ, a Palm Court, a theatre (modelled on Drury Lane) seating 3,000, a concert room seating 3,500 (which later became the roller skating rink), various museums and a variety of banqueting suites and refreshment facilities. The park was redesigned to include a trotting ring and cycle racing track (both within the horse racing course), a cricket ground, ornamental lakes, a Japanese village, tennis courts, a permanent fun fair and an open air swimming pool (next to the New River Reservoir).

110. Architect's drawing for the first Alexandra Palace. Illustrated London News, 20 February 1864.

WEST VIEW OF EXTERIOR OF PALACE

PLACE OF SAFETY FOR ART TREASURES RESCUED FROM EAST PICTURE GALLERY

BURNING OF CENTRAL TRANSEPT.—DESTRUCTION OF GRAND ORGAN AND ORCHESTRA

TAKING OUT THE LAST OF THE ART TREASURES JUST BEFORE THE DOORS WERE CLOS

111. *Destruction of the first Alexandra Palace, as portrayed by* The Graphic, *16 June 1873.*

THE JAPANESE VILLAGE

THE ITALIAN GARDEN

THE CONSERVATORY

112. *Scenes soon after the opening of the second Alexandra Palace, from* The Graphic, *12 June 1875.*

113. *The arrival of the Prince of Wales at Alexandra Palace in 1876.*

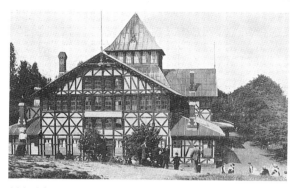

114. *The old banqueting hall in 1903, later known as the Blandford Hall, destroyed by fire in 1971. It was in the Park, to the east of the Palace.*

After more financial difficulties the Palace was closed for two years in 1889 and a part of the park to the north of the Palace was sold for building. The risk of further encroachment on the parklands led to a vigorous campaign spearheaded by Henry Burt, a prominent member of the Hornsey UDC, supported by Ralph Littler, Chairman of Wood Green UDC, which resulted in the Alexandra Palace and Park Act in 1900. This allowed Trustees, comprising representatives of Middlesex County Council and the local authorities of Hornsey, Wood Green, Islington, Tottenham, Friern Barnet and Finchley to buy the Park and Palace on behalf of the people in 1901. The purchase price was £150,000 of which Wood Green contributed £37,500. The Palace was reopened on 18 May 1901.

For most of the duration of the First World War the Palace and Park were closed and requisitioned to house German, Austrian and other internees and as a transit camp for Belgian refugees. Normal operations were restored in the 1920s but further financial problems arose in the '30s. In 1934 the BBC leased the east wing of the building and the first TV transmission was made on 2 Nov 1936 from the aerial erected on the south-east tower.

Both Palace and Park suffered some bomb damage during the Second World War and a restoration programme allowed the Palace to reopen in 1957. As a result of the 1963 London Government Act management of the Palace and Park passed to the Greater London Council in 1966. A GLC feasibility study proposing demolition of the Palace and the creation of a mammoth sports complex was not realised.

A GLC consultation exercise in 1974 confirmed that a large majority of Haringey residents wished to see the Palace and Park retained with improvements in management and amenities.

Haringey Council took over trusteeship in January 1980 with an £8m. dowry from the GLC. On 10 July in the same year the Palace was again seriously damaged by fire. The Great Hall, the banqueting suite and roller skating rink were completely gutted and most of the west wing severely damaged.

Haringey Council undertook the rebuilding of the Palace using the dowry and £42m insurance money. A temporary Alexandra Pavilion was erected on the former bowling green at the east end to house events during the rebuilding. Planning permission for converting most of the building as a major exhibition venue was granted in 1982 and rebuilding commenced in 1984.

The formal opening of the rebuilt Palace was on 17 March 1988 with a new Great Hall with a pitched roof without internal columns and a new West Hall replacing the Italian Gardens. The Palm Court had been restored to its past splendour with a new Phoenix Bar. Proposals for a hotel in the south-west frontage failed to materialise. Since reopening the Palace has again been home to many exhibitions and events. The Park had also been given a substantial face-lift with improved car-parking, and lighting and new furniture and facilities. Many new trees were planted on the south-facing slope to re-establish the earlier arboretum. In the east wing plans for the refurbishment of the Victorian theatre and former BBC TV studios have yet to be realised. An ice skating rink, in prefrence to a roller rink, was built in the former east concert hall and opened in July 1990.

115. *Advertisement card for the Palace.*

116. *The grand organ at the second Palace. It was designed and built by Henry Willis.*

117. *The swimming pool in Alexandra Park. It was located between the racecourse and the main line railway, now the site of the Nature Reserve.*

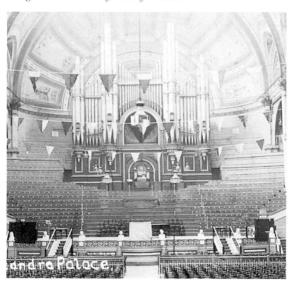

118. *Programme cover for the Boys Scouts' Rally at the Palace in 1922.*

At present Haringey Council is aiming to obtain legal authority to grant a long lease to a commercial consortium to run the Palace.

Although attempts by the council to have the Palace listed in 1978 failed, a further attempt in 1997 was successful resulting in a Grade II listing by English Heritage.

Alexandra Palace and Park have been the venue for an extremely wide range of events and celebrations. Firework displays originated by James Pain in 1875 have remained popular to this day. Balloon ascents and parachute jumpng were popular with the Victorian and Edwardian crowds. Large Scout rallies involving tens of thousands of young people were held in 1913, 1922 and 1930. The roller skating rink, opened

in 1901, survived until the 1970s and now ice-skating provides an alternative; a dry ski slope was popular in its time. The Park has seen pop concerts, beer festivals, cultural festivals, and fairgrounds as well as the more traditional sports of cricket, football, tennis and golf. Sports events are discussed in more detail on pp126-130.

The Alexandra Palace building was not always popular with commentators. One of the first, James Thorne in his *Handbook to the Environs of London* (1876), said:

> The new Alexandra Palace is a substantial structure of brick, iron, and glass, unnecessarily ugly externally, from whatever point it be viewed ...

And Thomas Burke in *The Outer Circle* (1921):

> I forgot to include among the features of Wood Green a large, four-square building of the type described as 'places of amusement'. It is called Alexandra Palace. It looks like it. It doesn't amuse me.

Martin S. Briggs in his *Middlesex Old and New* (1934) says:

> Lastly, there is Alexandra Palace, an offence to the eye for miles around and a heavy charge on the authorities ... Wood Green is overpowered and vulgarised by the Alexandra Palace.

R. Michael Robbins in his *New Survey of England* (1953), in describing Wood Green, says:

> It has no distiguishing feature except the deplorable Alexandra Palace scowling over it from a ridge running in from the west side ... To the W. the gigantic slothful bulk of the Alexandra Palace spoils the outlook.

At least one positive view was expressed by local-born Lord Ted Willis in his autobiography (1970) with the words:

> Alexandra Palace, a strange, fascinating, romantic place with its great halls, domed roofs, wide terraces and sweeping gardens.

Inns and Taverns

COACHING INNS

Wood Green's earliest inns were on the High Road to cater for stage-coaches, travellers, traders and drovers.

The first was the Three Jolly Butchers, established by 1781, on the west of the High Road, just south of the junction with Bounds Green Road and north of the New River which crossed the High Road at this point. It was an ideal location to catch the traffic to and from Enfield to the north and Friern Barnet and Whetstone to the north-west. The first proprietor was Thomas King, followed by Thomas Chambers and in 1810 by Alexander Watson. The Watson family retained ownership for several decades (*see* p33-34). With the presence of the pub this steep section of the High Road once known as Claybush Hill became known as Jolly Butchers Hill.

The Queen's Head, located just to the south of Duckett's Common, existed from 1794 when the first licensee was Samuel Wilkinson. From 1856, proprietor John Palmer ran an omnibus service to London and Winchmore Hill. Here he stabled horses for his own use and for the local fire brigade, but he seems to have overworked them. In 1869 one dropped dead pulling the Winchmore Hill bus and another died pulling the fire engine. As well as the traffic along Green

Lanes this inn was particularly well placed for visitors to Alexandra Palace and also had tea gardens. In 1876 the proprietor offered 'unusual facilities for refreshment to visitors to the Alexandra Palace, and to those who selected the favourite locality for pleasure and health.'

By 1800 these two inns were joined in the High Road by the Nags Head, on the southern corner of Station Road. The original building was a long sprawling establishment with livery stables.

VICTORIAN DRINKING PALACES

By 1900 all three of these coaching inns had been transformed into drinking palaces, adorned with cupolas and large outside lanterns, catering more for local needs. The Queen's Head was converted in 1898 and today still retains most of its late Victorian features. During its rebuilding in 1898 a solid gold ring of c.1400, inset with an emerald and an inscription in French, was found; it is now in the British Museum.

The Three Jolly Butchers became the Three Jolly Butchers Hotel in 1900 and survived until 1959 after which the site was redeveloped. The etched glass windows from the pub were offered to the Council by the developers and taken into storage by the Borough Engineer. A new Jolly Butchers pub then occupied the ground floor of a four-storey office building. In the early 1990s the trend of renaming long-established pubs was underway and The Jolly Butchers suffered its final indignity by becoming The Rat and Carrot.

119. The Three Jolly Butchers inn c.1890. It stood on the west side of the High Road, south of Bounds Green Road.

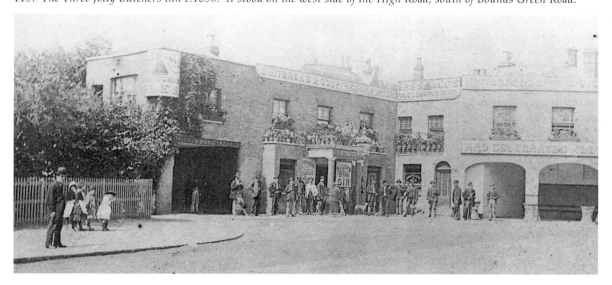

120. *The Nags Head inn, 1889. It was built c.1800 and reconstructed in 1900.*

121. *The Queen's Head Hotel, Green Lanes c.1916. This replaced a coaching inn at the turn of the century.*

122. *The Three Jolly Butchers Hotel c.1910, which replaced the former coaching inn. In its turn, the new building was demolished in 1959.*

It was again renamed Ganley's in 1998 by which time many north London pubs were in Irish ownership. The Nags Head underwent a face-lift in 1997 when it too suffered a name change, becoming The Goose and Granite.

ROADSIDE TAVERNS

As the population grew new taverns emerged. A beerhouse, the Jolly Anglers, was established in Station Road by 1840 for New River fishermen. It was rebuilt in 1905 and is today a reminder of the Edwardian past.

The Ranelagh Tavern had opened at Bounds Green by 1862, but restrictive temperance covenants prevented the building of public houses in Bowes Park and encouraged trade for the Springfield Park Tavern (1869) on the west side of Bounds Green Road. The Springfield became a popular folk music venue in the 1960s and '70s.

Solid, four-square taverns and hotels, occupying corner positions to which meeting rooms or halls were later attached, were a feature of the second half of the 19th century and they were much used by local societies and clubs. The Fishmongers Arms (1855) with the Bourne Hall attached, at the corner of Trinity Road, was built on the site of the former Wood Green Farm farmhouse and yard. Its exterior is hardly changed today, but it is now known as O'Rafferty's. The Nightingale Tavern (1866), a substantial building once with adjacent Masonic Hall and Assembly Rooms on the corner of Nightingale Road, is now reduced to a single storey building. The Kings Arms Hotel (1870) with its large assembly rooms on the corner of White Hart Lane remains, known in the 1990s as The Kings. Its former stable-yard, once able to accommodate 25 horses, became the entrance to the Stables Nite Club which occupied the assembly rooms. It has recently (June 2000) been refurbished as Charley Brown's. The Alexandra Park Tavern (c.1868) with adjacent tea gardens was opposite the junction of the High Road and Mayes Road. By 1910 the gardens were replaced by shops and the ground floor of the pub was extended. This pub survived until the development of Shopping City in the mid-1970s. At the southern end of the High Road at the corner with Turnpike Lane the Wellington had appeared by 1872 and retained its prominent corner position for over one hundred years. Today, the main part of the building is a Burger King restaurant but the pub itself lives on in reduced circumstances in one of its bars in Turnpike Lane.

123. *The Nightingale Hotel, High Road, c.1905.*

124. *The King's Arms and Assembly Rooms, High Road, c.1905.*

125. *The Alexandra Park Tavern, High Road, 1889, with adjacent tea gardens. It stood opposite Mayes Road.*

126. *The Fishmongers' Arms, High Street, c.1906. To the right stands the fire engine house, built in 1901.*

LOCALS

As estates were developed so 'local' pubs were built. Amongst the earliest were the Duke of Edinburgh (1868) in Mayes Road; the Alexandra Tavern (1868) in Commerce Road, one of the two surviving original buildings in that road; and the Prince of Wales (1868) in Trinity Road. These three are little changed externally and retain their original names. The first licensee of the Alexandra was Henry Oram, previously employed as a butler at Highfield House in Winchmore Hill. The tavern passed to his brother-in-law, Thomas Burry, in 1876 and in turn to his son and remained in the same family for several generations. The Freemasons Tavern and His Lordship's Tavern were on the north-side of Lordship Lane by 1875 and were probably much appreciated by the later residents of the nearby Noel Park Estate which was also subject to temperance restrictions. The Seven Oaks on the corner of Winkfield Road and White Hart Lane was in existence by the early 1890s.

Another good example of a late Victorian pub is the Starting Gate opposite the present Alexandra Palace railway station in Station Road. It began as the Palace Café in 1875, became a public house in 1896 and was refitted in 1899 by Richard Dickenson. Later renamed the Alexandra Palace and Railway Hotel it became the Starting Gate in 1958 recalling the Alexandra Park race-

127. The Salisbury Hotel, Green Lanes. Designed by J.C. Hill in 1889, it was the key building in the Grand Parade.

course. It was Grade II listed in 1990 and retains its original internal and external features including cast-iron columns, engraved glass screens and watercolour scenes with one of Alexandra Palace. It has recently become the home of the Two-Way Mirror Theatre Club which had previously been resident for several years at the Springfield Tavern.

The grandest example of a late Victorian public house in the area is the Salisbury Hotel, in Green Lanes, Harringay at the corner of St Ann's Road. It was part of the Grand Parade conceived by the developer J. C. Hill in 1898-99. He designed and built the Salisbury, not only providing spacious bars, but also a large billiard room, restaurant and concert hall. Hill had also built the Queen's at Crouch End in similar style. The Salisbury was refurbished in 1997-8, highlighting some of its earlier splendour.

More recently new pubs or bars have been established in former shops. One of the first of these, in the 1960s was the Nelson, now renamed Rattle and Hum, on the corner of Cranbrook Park and the High Road, in a former florist's shop. The Palace Gates and the Park Inn are in old shops in Crescent Road as is Henley's Bar in Myddleton Road.

128. The Seven Oaks in White Hart Lane, c.1905.

129. *A weatherboarded general shop in Station Road, 1903, looking west towards Alexandra Palace. This shop was recorded in 1837 as was the row of cottages adjacent and the original Jolly Anglers Inn beyond them.*

Village Shop to Shopping City

Wood Green's first shop, a general stores, was recorded in 1798 and located near the top of Jolly Butchers Hill. At least one other shop had appeared by 1837 on the south side of Station Road between the Nags Head and Jolly Anglers inns. The growth of retail shops initially followed the needs of an expanding local population but the potential of the High Road as a major north London shopping centre had been realised by the turn of the 20th century.

SHOPPING STREETS
The first shopping streets were laid out as part of the Wood Green Estate, to the north of St Michael's Church in the early 1860s. These were the appropriately named Commerce Road and Finsbury Road, which intersected it. By 1868 there were 22 shops in Commerce Road and fourteen in Finsbury Road which included virtually every type of business. By 1884, when the

roads were fully occupied, Commerce Road held 53 shops and Finsbury Road another thirty. A small parade of shops was also built along Trinity Road between Finsbury and Commerce Roads by 1890.

Many of these survived until the Second World War but after that, war damage, the competition of the High Road, and the very age of some of the properties began to take its toll. and by the late 1950s many traditional retail shops had given way to small manufacturing operations. Redevelopment in the 1960s swept away all the original shops in Commerce Road, and in the 1970s Finsbury Road was truncated and all the shops on the east side disappeared. Only the small parade of houses and shops on the west side between Commerce and Nightingale Roads remains, of which only two shops are a legacy of Wood Green's original shopping centre. One business, King Brothers, ironmongers, established in 1884, still survives at its corner shop at no. 51 Finsbury Road.

By the mid-1880s another shopping street, Myddleton Road, was emerging about a half a mile further north in Bowes Park. Beginning with four shops in 1884, there were 39 in 1894 and eighty by 1912 by which time the road was

130. *Ashby's greengrocery in Commerce Road, c.1920.*

131. *Myddleton Road, c.1905, looking towards Whittington Road and Bowes Park Station.*

complete. A further twenty or so shops were established in nearby Whittington Road. In 1957 Myddleton Road could still boast six major provision stores, including a Co-op, Home & Colonial, and Gunners; four butchers; five greengrocers and two bakers. These streets retain their Victorian appearance almost intact, but as a result of competition from the High Road, and more recently from the growth of superstores, several of the traditional businesses have given way to non-retail enterprises and some shops are converted to residential use.

Some Victorian housing estates were provided with local shopping terraces or parades. Examples of these are St Michaels Terrace (*c*.1870), opposite Alexandra Palace Station, and Crescent Road (1898). Shops on the north side of Lordship Lane, to serve the Pellatt Grove and Winkfield and Acacia Road areas, and in Springfield Terrace on the west side of Bounds Green Road adjacent to the Springfield Park Tavern, were built by 1890.

THE HIGH ROAD

Development of the High Road as a shopping thoroughfare began between White Hart Lane and Truro Road. In 1868 when it was known as the Southgate Road there were nine shops and by the early 1880s, when it was completed and known as High Street, there were 45 small businesses. A few of the shops on the east side between Kings Road and Canning Crescent and a parade on the west between Nightingale and Truro Roads remain today but the remainder on the west side have been redeveloped.

The parade of shops on the east side of Jolly Butchers Hill, once known as Hardy Terrace, date from 1880. Part of this terrace was replaced by Wood Green Underground Station in 1932, but the remainder of the terrace survives.

The increase in shops on the High Road south from Jolly Butchers Hill to Turnpike Lane kept pace with the progress of the housing estates. The first shopping parades on the west side of the High Road were established by 1880 between the GER railway bridge and Mayes Road, known as Market Terrace, and between Mayes Road and Brampton Park Road; these being part of the

132. *Early shops in the part of High Road then known as Jolly Butchers Hill, c.1910. It shows a baker's and Wood Green's first post office, dating from the 1860s.*

133. *High Road, c.1910. View from Mayes Road looking north. Wood Green's first department store, Edmonds Bros., is on the right.*

134. *Shops in the High Road between White Hart Lane and Truro Road c.1904. This section was once known as High Street.*

135. Lymington Avenue, 1910. The shops at the left are now replaced by the Shopping City complex. The gardens to the right belong to Dovecote Villas, which were replaced by the Cheapside shopping parade in 1911.

Park Ridings Estate. Market Terrace, with its open-fronted greengrocer's and fishmonger's, survived virtually unchanged until the development of the Shopping City in the late 1970s.

Shops between Brampton Park Road and Coleraine Road were built as part of the Coleraine Estate between 1890-1900 and others between Coleraine Road and Turnpike Lane by the 1880s.

On the east side between the railway and Gladstone Avenue is Gladstone Terrace, a shopping parade built in the first phase of the Noel Park Estate in the mid-1880s. Further south on the same side between the former Noel Park Road and Lymington Avenue stood the Alexandra Park Tavern and its adjacent tea gardens with a small parade of shops on either side. By 1900 this section was redeveloped to include Wood Green's first large store, Edmonds Brothers, the drapers, which occupied a large part of this block.

By the late 1880s the Artisans', Labourers' and General Dwellings Co. had built two parades either side of Dovecote Avenue as part of their Noel Park Estate, replacing earlier mid-Victo-rian villas. By 1911 they had also built the Cheapside shopping parade, extending south from Lymington Avenue with the prominent entrance to the Empire Theatre at its centre and the distinctive domed turrets at each end of the parade.

SHOPPING CENTRE
By the turn of the 20th century the High Road was attracting shoppers from further afield, especially from Harringay and Hornsey.

The early Victorian villas between Dovecote Avenue and Turnpike Lane, which had large front gardens were the next target for developers and as early as 1901 single-storey shops were erected over the gardens of some. Today's shops between Whymark Avenue and Turnpike Lane are typical of such development and the upper floors of some of the Victorian villas can still be seen.

By 1910 national stores such as the grocers Sainsbury's and Lipton's, Ridgeway's tea merchants, Home & Colonial Stores and Lilley and

136. *Dovecote Villas on the east side of the High Road, in 1910 prior to development of the Cheapside shopping parade.*

137. *Cheapside Parade, High Road in 1922, with the Empire Theatre centre stage.*

138. View of the High Road north from Coleraine Road in 1960, showing Barton's and other department stores.

Skinner's bootmakers were interspersed with local merchants on the west side. On the east side were three large drapery stores, Barton's (nos. 28-32, having acquired Thomas & Co. at nos. 30-32), Edmonds (nos. 88-90 and 102-112) and Denham & Gaydor (114-120), occupying the sites of the large villas. Edmonds later acquired Denham & Gaydor. The growth of Barton's was particularly spectacular. It began in 1906 and expanded to nos. 28-32 by 1910, 26-34a by 1921 and 26-36 by 1925, when it erected its wide-fronted store with a colonnaded upper-storey which made a distinctive contrast to its late-Victorian neighbours.

Newcomers in the late 1920s included Woolworth's, Marks & Spencer's, Barratt's Shoes, Dorothy Perkins ladies' outfitters, Saxone Shoes and Bon Marché ladies' outfitters.

The last sections of the High Road to be developed in the 1930s were at each end of the west side. Broadway Parade was constructed between the Palace Gates railway line and the Nags Head. on the site of Gladstone Gardens. This included the entrance to the Gaumont Palace cinema whose auditorium was built on the site of The Elms in 1934. The remaining villas between Turnpike

Lane and Coleraine Road were demolished in the late 1920s and by 1932 a new parade was built which included the art-deco building of the tailor, Montague Burton, with a Temperance billiard hall above, and the Times Furnishing Co. store.

In 1932 the Piccadilly line opened stations at Wood Green and Turnpike Lane and the High Road, already well served by trams and buses, became one of the most accessible and largest of north London shopping streets, rivalling Tottenham High Road. It went largely unscathed during the last war and some of the large stores on the east side were modernised in the 1950s. These included Barton's, with a new square tower, but this store was closed after a serious fire in the 1960s. Its site is now occupied by the British Gas Energy Centre and British Home Stores. In the 1950s, the two Edmonds stores on the corner of Lymington Avenue and the former Noel Park Road were replaced by the London Co-operative Society departmental store.

In the side streets off the main road, such as Lymington Avenue, Mayes Road (once the location of the People's Market), Dovecote Avenue etc., stood various colourful market stalls, a few of which remain to this day.

139. Shopping City in 1984.

140. Shopping City c.1985.

THE SHOPPING CITY

By 1976 Wood Green was the largest shopping centre in north London, with a turnover of in excess of £20m. The key factor in its expansion after that and the bulding of Shopping City was the closure in 1963 of the LNER Palace Gates branch line. This released a wide swathe of land cutting diagonally across the High Road, including Noel Park station and a goods yard.

The Wood Green Shopping City, designed by Shepperd Robson and Partners, was opened by HM The Queen on 13 May 1981. The red-brick complex is built on both sides of the High Road with integrated multi-storey car parking. The shopping areas are on the ground and first floors, with a connecting walkway across the High Road at first floor level, with residential accomodation for 220 people on a higher deck. The casualties in the construction were Market Terrace on the west side and Alexandra Park Tavern and the Co-operative Society site on the east as well as smaller shops; the displaced traders were offered sites in a new Market Hall within the complex.

Many of the old High Road shops have gone and new names have moved in, but Wood Green remains an important shopping centre despite the rival attractions of Brent Cross Shopping Centre and out-of-town malls.

141. Horse-trams in the High Road, c.1901.

A Hub of Transport

COACHES AND HORSES

From the latter half of the 18th century horse-drawn traffic had the advantage of travelling on the improved roads created by the Turnpike Trusts. One of these was Green Lanes (including the High Road in Wood Green), extending from Wood Green to Bush Hill Park in Enfield. This was controlled, from 1739, by the Stamford Hill and Green Lanes Turnpike Trust, which had a toll gate at the junction with Turnpike Lane.

By 1825 there were up to five daily short-stage coach return journeys between Southgate and London via Wood Green and at least one commercial waggoner provided a daily service from the City to Wood Green.

Horse-drawn buses, carrying up to twenty passengers inside, were introduced into London by George Shillibeer in 1829 and quickly became popular. As the surburban population increased, so enterprising innkeepers ran horse-bus services from outlying districts into the City. these included John Palmer, proprietor of the Queen's Head just south of Duckett's Common, who on 13 October 1856, took delivery of an omnibus for his service to London Bridge. In 1870 he ran eighteen daily services to London via Manor House in addition to more frequent services from Edmonton and Tottenham. Also, the 'Enterprise' Omnibus operated five daily runs from West Green to Dalston.

But the financial viability of horse buses in London was reduced by railways and then further by horse trams, which could carry more passengers. These were introduced in the area by the North London Tramways Co. in 1852 and the first local service, from Seven Sisters to Edmonton, began in 1872 and was extended to Finsbury Park in 1885. Two years later rails were laid from Manor House to Wood Green and in December 1887 cumbersome steam-powered trams, with their separate locomotive, were introduced on this route. It was extended to Earlham Grove, then the location of the Wood Green Local Board offices (later the Town Hall) but steam trams proved unpopular on account of dirt and noise and were withdrawn. In 1891 North London Tramways were sold to North Metropolitan Tramways and horse-power was re-introduced and a new depot built on the site of Wood Green bus garage. This depot became and remains the hub of local transport for north London.

142. *Steam tram at Wood Green in 1890.*

ELECTRIC TRAMS AND TROLLEYBUSES

Wood Green was home to the first electric tramway in London, the Alexandra Park Electric Railway, a short route between the east gate of the park up to the Palace. It was, however, short-lived, running from May 1898 until September 1899.

Electrification of the former horse tramways began at the turn of the 20th century by Metropolitan Electric Tramways in collaboration with Middlesex County Council. The Wood Green depot was converted for electric traction early in 1904, accommodating 62 cars, expanding to 87 by 1908. It soon became the focus of several routes in all directions: to Finsbury Park via Manor House (July 1904); Bruce Grove via Lordship Lane (August 1904); Alexandra Palace via Station Road (April 1906); to the Ranelagh Tavern, Bounds Green Road (November 1906), extending to New Southgate (May 1907) and Finchley via Woodhouse Road (April 1909); to Palmers Green (June 1907), Winchmore Hill (August 1908) and ultimately Enfield (July 1909). From 1912 through journeys to central London were possible through inter-connection with the LCC tramway system at Finsbury Park.

Electric trams were gradually replaced by electric trolleybuses between 1936 and 1939 by the London Passenger Transport Board. Once again the Wood Green depot was restructured for the new vehicles and in 1938 housed over 100 of them. The routes were essentially the same as those for the trams. Trolleybuses survived until 1961 when they were replaced by diesel motor buses and the Wood Green depot once again altered. The depot is now operated by Arriva for London Buses.

THE INDEPENDENTS

Petrol motor bus routes ran through Wood Green from 1912 when the London General Omnibus Co. (LGOC) extended its no. 29 route from Wood Green to Southgate and Cockfosters.

The era of independent motor-bus operators began ten years later. They were attracted to the suburban areas and to the no. 29 route in particular. Consequently a number of them were based in the Wood Green area. Five operators possessing seven buses were housed at the Whymark Garage in Whymark Avenue between 1923-24. This later became second-hand car showrooms and remains today in commercial use. The Empire Garage in Boreham Road housed three operators in 1925 and is now occupied by a building contractor. The Syree Brothers' Garage

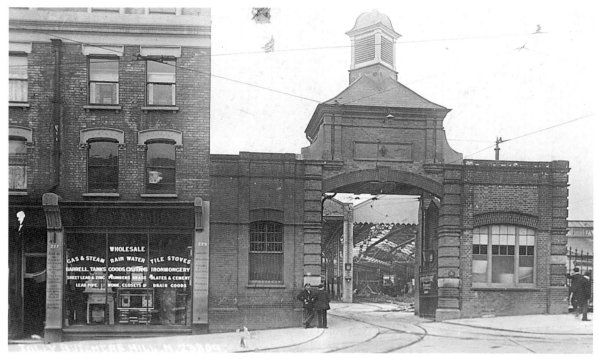

143. *Tram depot in the High Road, c.1910.*

144. *The first electric tram from Wood Green to Bruce Castle, 1904.*

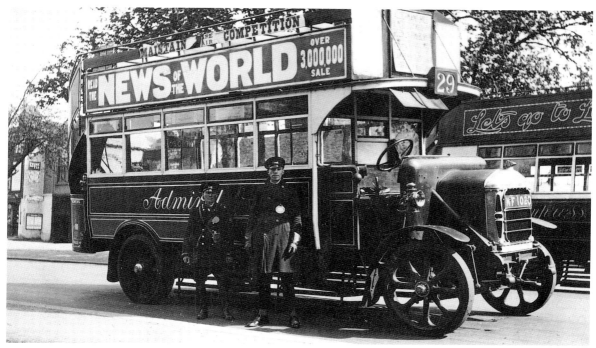

145. An Admiral bus on the 29 route c.1925.

at nos. 7-9 Commerce Road housed seven operators between 1924-31. It remained a garage until the redevelopment of the 1970s when housing occupied the site. Each operator had its own distinctive livery and name. The latter included the 'Empress', 'Newstead', 'Empire', 'Empire's Best', 'The Lancastrian', 'Reliance', 'The Leader' and 'Admiral'. With the exception of the 'Admiral' most of them were one- or two-man affairs, their proprietors being local men and some former LGOC drivers or conductors.

The Admiral fleet was the most successful on the no. 29 route in direct competition with the London General Omnibus Company. Introduced by Bernard Cosgrove of Palmers Green, the first Admirals ran in 1922, out of a garage in Willow Walk, West Green, being part of the engineering works of A.T. Bennett & Co. Ltd. Bennett, a local business man, also provided buses on the route, and became sole proprietor of the 'Admiral' fleet in 1925. He introduced a no. 29 daily service to Hadley Wood and a 'Fair Fares' campaign in 1923 which offered cheaper tickets than the General company. The no. 29 was the principal Admiral route but it operated on other services such as nos. 58, 201, 280 and 529. In August 1927,

with a fleet of 37 buses, Bennett formed a new company, the London Public Omnibus Co. Ltd, which attracted a number of smaller operators under its umbrella, but this came under the control of the LGOC in March 1928. The creation of the London Passenger Transport Board in 1933 saw the end of the private bus operators. West Green bus garage remained operational until 1962 when the fleet was transferred to Wood Green depot.

Alfred Temple Bennett (1879-1969) had strong Wood Green connections, particularly with St James's Presbyterian Church where he attended the Sunday School and where he was married in 1906. He was a Middlesex JP and served on the Wood Green Juvenile Bench in the late 1930s. From 1928 he lived in Winchmore Hill.

DAYS AT THE SEASIDE

'Empire's Best' coaches, run by the Webber Brothers of Hornsey, operated from Boreham Road garage in 1925 on the no. 294 route and later on the no. 69. In 1926 they moved to Syree's Garage in Commerce Road and sold out to the City Motor Bus Co. Ltd. in 1928 to concentrate

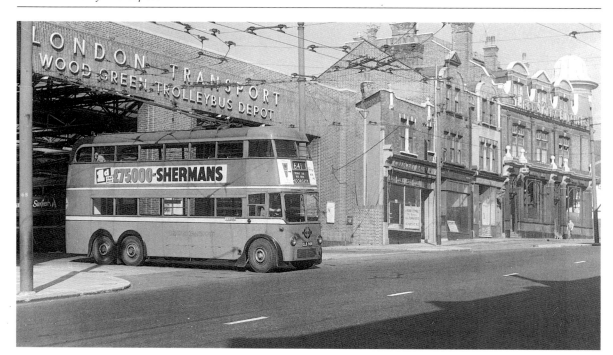

146. *(Top) One of the last trolleybuses leaving Wood Green Depot, c.1960.*

147. *(Below) Eastern National Bus Depot, Lordship Lane, 1958.*

on their London-Clacton daily coach service, operating from 44 Commerce Road until the 1960s.

Other independent motor coach companies also found Wood Green, and Lordship Lane in particular, a good location for services to the east coast. A coach station and garage once existed at 727 Lordship Lane, next to the Congregational Church. This was established by the City Omnibus Co. in the 1920s for its Wood Green-Southend service. From 1929 to 1934 it was operated by Westcliff Motor Services Ltd. with whom the City had a shared timetable. The building was sold in 1934 to the City Coach Co. Ltd and in 1938 was the home of Orange Luxury Coaches. Post-war it became an Eastern National coach station and more recently part of the site was occupied by a W.H. Smith 'Do-it-all' centre and is now a Mecca Bingo Hall.

UNDERGROUND CONNECTIONS

In 1932 Wood Green's public transport connections were enlarged with the extension of the Piccadilly Line from Finsbury Park to Cockfosters. Turnpike Lane, Wood Green and Bounds Green Underground stations were opened in September as part of the first phase of the extension to Arnos Grove; the final section including Southgate, Enfield West (now Oakwood) and Cockfosters was completed the following year. The station facades, booking halls and platforms, designed by Charles Holden, brought more art deco architecture to Wood Green.

The Making of a Borough

PARISH ADMINISTRATION

From the early 16th century the parish of All Hallows, Tottenham was divided into four wards: High Cross, Middle, Nether (later Lower) and Wood Green, each with comparable populations. In area the more rural Wood Green ward was roughly the sum of the other three and effectively covered the western half of the parish. According to Bedwell in 1631, Wood Green ward included 'Westgreene, Hangers [Hanger Lane], Dou'cotes [Ducketts], Chapman-greene, Woodgreene, the Hill, Tottenham Wood and Boundesbrooke.' The area of the ward was 2074 acres.

Until 1887 the ward boundaries remained unchanged. Increasingly, local administration moved from the old manorial courts to the parish vestry meetings which dealt with poor relief and the maintenance of highways. They also appointed parish officials, such as constables, churchwardens, overseers of the poor, surveyors of the highways, the beadle and the bread and ale tasters.

ENCLOSURES

One subject dealt with frequently by Tottenham Vestry was the enclosure of waste and common land; this had been formerly dealt with by the manorial court. The parish of Tottenham was not subject to the Enclosure Acts which applied in neighbouring Edmonton (1801) and Hornsey (1812) due to the absence of common fields by this time and probably on account of the relatively small extent of waste lands. Nevertheless, 'commoners' enjoyed the 'rights of common' on Wood Green Common and elsewhere and were likely to object to gradual encroachment on these open lands. After 1773, applications for small-scale enclosure were generally agreed subject to a yearly payment to the parish poor fund. The earlier building of houses on Wood Green Common and the creation of tracks across it had to be accepted as a *de facto* situation since no records had been kept. However, new illegal enclosure was dealt with less sympathetically and the offending walls, fences and hedges were pulled down. In 1793 Edward Wyburd, a prominent landowner and member of the Vestry, attempted to seek registration of encroachments on common land with a view to regularising the situation. There was much prevarication, resulting in a resolution dated 4 October 1794:

148. A function of parish vestries each year or two was to walk the bounds of the parish to check that boundary marks were in position and that no encroachments had taken place. The illustration depicts Tottenham Vestry assembled for this purpose outside the Alexandra Palace c.1880, at the Tottenham boundary with Hornsey.

Resolved that no building or inclosure whatsover in future be permitted upon any part of the Waste or Common Lands of this Parish without an Application shall be allowed at a meeting of the Vestry for the specific purpose ...

From 1818 a Waste Lands Book was kept by the Vestry. However, such enclosure as did take place was relatively modest and Wood Green still benefits from a large amount of common land later converted to public open spaces.

TOTTENHAM LOCAL BOARD OF HEALTH (1850-1888)

Tottenham was one of the first parishes to seek the establishment of a local board of health under the Public Health Act of 1848 and this was achieved in 1850. The Board took responsibility for highways, lighting (1858) and fire fighting (1869). In 1887 Tottenham was divided into six wards; High Cross, Middle, Lower, St Ann's, West Green and Wood Green and at this time Wood Green ward was reduced to 1460 acres, its southern boundary being defined by the Moselle river east to Gladstone Road, Brook Road, and Lordship Lane and its eastern boundary ran due north from Hatherley Road. It contained 2350 houses with a population of 15,230 but did not include the emerging Noel Park Estate which was then in West Green ward.

The responsibility for the local fire-fighting services became a vexed issue in 1867 when the Wood Green Ratepayers requested their own engine. In October 1868 Tottenham Vestry granted land adjacent to St Michael's Church on which to build an engine house and a new fire engine was purchased. But in February 1869 the Local Board claimed control of the engine and its house much to the displeasure of the Wood Green Volunteer Fire Brigade. As a result, John Kidd, then Chairman of the Wood Green Ratepayers, impounded the fire engine in his own carriage house, his action being supported by 150 ratepayers. The matter was resolved six months later when it was agreed that while the Local Board would have control they accepted the offer of the Wood Green Volunteers to maintain and operate the fire services there.

TOWARDS SEPARATION

As the suburbs of Tottenham and Wood Green grew so emerged differences in their social mix and character. In Tottenham the flatter terrain allowed the building of higher density terraced housing for rent, and the cheap-day Great Eastern Railway tickets attracted working men and artisans to the area. In contrast, the early Wood Green developers offered villa-type and more spacious properties to a larger proportion of owner-occupiers. This, coupled with higher railway fares on the GNR, attracted a wealthier class of resident such as middle managers, office managers, supervisors, teachers, civil servants etc.

The aspirations of the more vocal Wood Green residents were channelled through the Wood Green Ratepayers' Association which began a campaign for separation from Tottenham in 1867. A meeting held at the Fishmongers' Arms on 4 February 1869 complained that:

they [Tottenham Local Board] had at the present time many things to do, but had no money to do them with'.

The inadequacy of drainage and the state of the roads in Wood Green were a particular cause for concern. It was suggested by a Mr Robbins that: 'they [Wood Green] could separate from Tottenham and he thought if they did so they would be much better off (to the accompaniment of cheers).' Another speaker said: 'It was time some steps were taken, for Wood Green seems to be looked on as a sort of cash box for the rest of the parish.'

Indeed, the Poor Rates paid by Wood Green ward (£3094 for half-year, 1868) were double those of any other ward in the parish.

At that time the nine members of the Tottenham Local Board were elected from the five ecclesiastical districts of All Hallows (3), Holy Trinity (3), St Michael's, Wood Green (1), St Paul's (1) and St Ann's (1). In March 1869 Wood Green recommended increasing the Local Board to twelve members with St Michael's returning two of them. This was achieved in 1871 and the Local Board membership was further increased to eighteen in 1887. Wood Green's increased representation on the Board was to be a stepping-stone on the road to complete separation.

149. Sir Ralph Littler, C.B., QC. First Chairman of Wood Green Local Board (1888-94) and Urban District Council (1894-1900).

WOOD GREEN LOCAL BOARD OF HEALTH (1888-1894)

It was to be almost two decades before Wood Green secured its independence with the creation of the Wood Green Local Board of Health on 29 September 1888. Then the south-eastern extent of the district was altered again to include the whole of the Noel Park Estate with the boundary along Westbury Avenue and a line due north from Lordship Lane to Devonshire Hill. The area was now 1625 acres with a population of 23,000.

Board offices were established at Earlham Grove House in 1890, where Wood Green's first public library was established in 1892 and a public telephone office by the turn of the century.

The first chairman of the Wood Green Local Board was (Sir) Ralph Littler QC, once resident in Clarence Road, who had been prominent in the campaign for separation. He had cut his teeth over a decade earlier in the successful campaign to separate Southgate from Edmonton in a situation which had some parallels with that of Wood

Green. Littler also served on the Middlesex County Council as its chairman and was also chairman of the Middlesex Quarter Sessions. In 1891 he co-sponsored the proposal that the County Council together with neighbouring local authorities should purchase Alexandra Palace and Park. Although this was not achieved until 1900 it was an important issue for the fledgling Wood Green Local Board to deal with. Wood Green's contribution to the purchase was £37,500.

WOOD GREEN COTTAGE HOSPITAL

An early decision of the Board was to support the building of the Passmore Edwards Cottage Hospital, later known as the Wood Green and Southgate Hospital. It stood at the corner of Bounds Green Road and Gordon Road, the land having been bought from the Ecclesiastical Commissioners, once being part of the Bowes Manor estate. The cost of the building, £2,300, was mainly borne by the Passmore Edwards Foundation, on condition that 'Wood Green would maintain it and if there were a large working class population in Wood Green.' The latter condition was fulfilled with the reinstatement of the Noel Park Estate in the Wood Green district in 1888. The hospital was designed by Charles Ball, and the foundation stone laid by Passmore Edwards himself on 25 August 1894. It was opened by his wife on 15 June 1895 with a male and female ward each of four beds, operating theatre, convalescent rooms and staff accommodation. Patients were accepted from Wood Green, Hornsey and Southgate. The hospital was enlarged to 25 beds in 1904, to 30 in 1911 and to 52 in 1922. The last expansion was known as the Sports Extension in tribute to local sports people who had raised funds for the hospital. By 1927 an X-ray department and other

150. Passmore Edwards (later Wood Green) Cottage Hospital in Bounds Green Road c.1910.

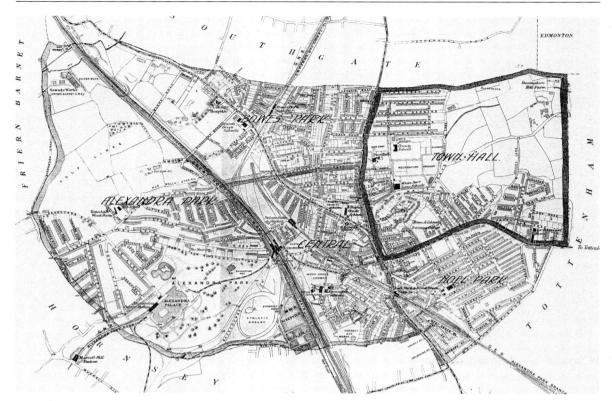

151. The area administered by the Wood Green Urban District Council in 1913. This map shows the civic ward boundaries at that time.

facilities were added. In 1948 the hospital became part of the National Health Service and in 1974 it came under the control of the Enfield and Haringey Area Health Authority. Closure proposals in 1979 were stalled by local campaigns but as a result of staff reductions only 24 beds were operational. Control passed to the Haringey Health Authority in 1982 and the hospital was finally closed in 1985. The site has since been redeveloped and now includes the Bounds Green Health Centre.

THE LOCAL PRESS

Local newspapers took a keen interest in political and social issues; Council meetings were reported verbatim in its early days. The first to cover Wood Green was the *Tottenham and Edmonton Advertiser* which began as a monthly in 1855 by George Coventry, becoming the *Weekly Advertiser* from 1881 and later owned by George Crusha. The *Tottenham and Edmonton Weekly Herald* appeared in 1861 and was acquired by Crusha in 1864. The *Wood Green Weekly Herald*

began in 1890. The Heralds continued into the 1980s when the titles were taken over by the *Hornsey Journal*, and the *Weekly Herald* is now a freebie. The *Hornsey Journal* itself began in 1879 concentrating on Hornsey, but after the creation of Haringey has published special editions for various parts of the borough.   Other shorter-lived newspapers were the *North London and Wood Green Chronicle* (1890-7), the *Wood Green Sentinel* (at least 1909-37) and the *Wood Green Observer* (later 1930s-1950s). In the 1930s Bowes Park could boast its own *BowesPark Weekly News*.

WOOD GREEN URBAN DISTRICT COUNCIL (1894-1933)

The Wood Green Local Board had a short life, for in 1894 Wood Green became an Urban District Council – by 1891 the population had risen in ten years from 9381 to 25830. The new authority had wider powers over planning, highways, sewerage and drainage, public health, parks and open spaces and they were readily exercised.

152. *The Wood Green Town Hall in 1906. This was the former Earlham Grove House. It became Wood Green UDC offices in 1890 and Town Hall in 1894.*

PUBLIC SERVICES

Earlham Grove House and eleven acres of the surrounding land had been bought by the Board in 1893. The house became Wood Green Town Hall in 1894 and the grounds Town Hall Park, now known as Woodside Park. In 1913 the building was enlarged with a single-storey south wing to house the council chamber and a magistrates' court.

The new UDC was to oversee the final stages of the residential development of the area, to extend public amenities and to make the first provision for council housing (see pp55-56).

As we have seen above, from 1869 the Wood Green Volunteer Fire Brigade had its engine-house on the north side of Bounds Green Road next to St Michael's Infants School. By 1901 a new engine house was located on the High Road next to the Fishmongers Arms and in 1914 a new fire station, designed by C. H. Croxford, the Borough Engineer, costing £5,893, was built for the UDC in Bounds Green Road. Opened on 28 March, this station had an engine-house, training tower and initially six firemen's flats, a further six being built in 1924. A motor ambulance was also operated. The local fire service became part

153. *The opening of the Town Hall Extension in September 1913.*

154. A reception to mark the opening of the new fire station in Bounds Green Road on 28 March, 1914.

155. Members of Wood Green UDC in 1933. F.W. Locke JP (wearing chain of office) was the Chairman.

of the Middlesex Fire and Ambulance Service and then in 1965 it was integrated into the London Fire Brigade. The fire station itself became redundant in 1963 with the building of new fire stations at Hornsey, Southgate and Tottenham, after which it was converted into an Ambulance Station.

Perhaps the most distinctive building to be erected during the early years of the UDC was the Wood Green Public Library, which replaced the modest library in the Town Hall. Located at the corner of Station Road and the High Road, the dark red-brick building with its cupola and clock, was opened on 28 September 1907. Built at a cost of £8,569, a gift of the Andrew Carnegie Foundation, it remained a local landmark until 1973 when it was demolished to make way for a featureless office block typical of that era. A new Central Public Library, built by Haringey Council, was opened alongside Shopping City in 1979.

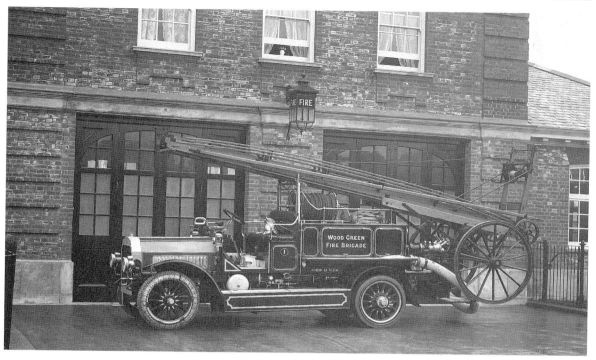

156. *Wood Green Fire Brigade's new tender, 1919.*

157. *Opening of Wood Green Library, 28 September 1907.*

158. Wood Green Library, 1908.

RECREATION AND LEISURE

The UDC was very protective of its open spaces which comprised about one-fifth of the area of the district. Following the policy initiated by the Local Board, most of them, formerly either waste or common land, were laid out as public gardens or recreation grounds, provided with amenities and most enclosed by railings. In 1906 there were 212 acres of open space consisting of 176 acres common and waste lands (including 154 acres of Alexandra Park), 21 acres of enclosed spaces and 9 acres leased from other bodies. By 1908 parts of Wood Green Common itself had been divided into Avenue Gardens, and a recreation ground (in Station Road) and a formal garden. Roads, with wide verges, such as Bounds Green Road, were lined with trees. The open spaces created by the tunnelling of the New River were leased from the New River Company and laid out to create Finsbury and Nightingale Gardens. In 1908 the UDC purchased 26 acres of land in White Hart Lane from the New River Company

to form a recreation ground. The Town Hall Park mentioned above had a bowling green and bandstand and there was also Trinity Gardens and Crescent Gardens. In fact, all the public gardens were featured in the picture postcards of the time. In 1930 66 acres were acquired north and south of White Hart Lane for allotments, playing fields and gardens; part of these was added to the New River Playing Fields. By 1933 there were 342 acres of open space, of which the UDC controlled just over half, the remainder including part of the Muswell Hill Golf Course, Scout Park and New River Company land being in private hands.

The provision of permanent allotments began by 1911 with sites at Hatherley Road (40 plots), Wolves Lane and at Chitts Hill (98) and by 1922 there were 628 with an additional 299 on the former Bounds Green Farm land and others at Devonshire Hill and Trinity Gardens.

An open-air swimming pool existed in Alexandra Park (*see* p88), between the New River

159. *(Top left) The bandstand in Town Hall Gardens (now Woodside Park) in 1903.*

160. *(Below) Western Road Baths, opened in 1911.*

161. *(Top right) The opening of Stuart Villa Day Nursery and Clinic in Stuart Crescent on 6 July, 1918. In the top row from right to left are J. Rushforth, Education Secretary, the Rev. C.G.A. Midwinter, Cllr J. Gilbert, chairman of the Maternity Committee and R. Farrell, Vice Chairman of the Education Committee. In the bottom row are Mrs A. Barratt, the opener, Cllr the Rev. D.J. Thomas, Chairman of the Education Committee and F. Pewtt Ridge, speaker.*

Reservoir and the racecourse from 1875 but its cleanliness was often called into question. Despite this it remained in use until 1907 when it was redesigned by the UDC to provide a 185 x 40ft pool which remained in use until the last war. Wood Green's first and only indoor swimming pool and public baths, in Western Road, designed by Harold Burgess, opened on 10 August 1911, on part of the former Moat Cottage site. They were closed in 1997 and converted to a banqueting suite. Another part of this site was taken for the construction of a refuse destructor, opened with much civic pomp in 1908. It is now the location of a recycling centre.

MUNICIPAL BOROUGH (1933-1965)

Wood Green made its first application for incorporation as a Borough Council as early as 1909, but this was unsuccessful. Its next attempt in 1933 was successful and its Charter of Incorporation (26 June 1933) as the Muncipal Borough of Wood Green, within the County of Middlesex, was presented by The Lord Mayor of London, Sir Percy Greenaway, on Charter Day, 20 September. The event was followed by four days of celebrations.

The population of the new borough was now 54,000 divided into three wards: Alexandra-Bowes, Noel Park and Town Hall each returning six Councillors. These together with six Aldermen comprised the new Council.

One of the Council's first decisions of the new Council was to approve the building of the open-air Olympic size swimming pool on the Albert Road Recreation Ground, which opened in 1934.

In 1935 it was agreed to build a new Town Hall on the Earlham Grove site. An open architectural competition was won by Sir John Brown and A.E. Henson & Partners for a building in traditional style. However, the project was set aside with the outbreak of war and afterwards the Council invited Sir John Brown and Co. to submit new plans for a site on the High Road then occupied by the Fishmongers' & Poulterers' Almshouses. The foundation stone was laid in April 1956, and the opening ceremony of the

163. *Arms of the Borough of Wood Green, assigned in September 1933. The motto* Nostrum Viret Robur *is a play on words, allowing interpetation as 'Wood Green Flourishes' or 'Our strength is as a Green Tree'.*

Civic Centre was performed by Mrs Joyce Butler MP on 15 March 1958. The building itself was to be the only civic centre built in the London area during the 1950s to a contemporary design.

Up to and including wartime the Council was controlled by Independents with a strong influence from the Ratepayers' Association. Between 1945-47 control passed to Labour, to be followed by an Independent/Conservative majority between 1947-49 and a return to Labour in 1949.

In 1965 Wood Green became part of the new London Borough of Haringey.

162. *The open-air swimming baths attached to the Albert Road Recreation Ground in Durnsford Road, 1935. The baths were closed in the 1990s and the building is now a garden centre.*

164. *The new Civic Centre at Wood Green in 1958.*

165. *Cllr Mrs Joyce Butler, MP, speaking at the opening ceremony of the Wood Green Civic Centre on 15 March 1958. Alderman A.G. Kendall is to the right.*

CIVIC CELEBRATIONS

Early in the life of the Council came the coronation of King George VI in May 1937. This was marked by many local events. The public gardens, the War Memorial and St Michael's Church were floodlit and the Tottenham Gas Company's showrooms in Bounds Green Road were illuminated by gas flares. The shopping streets were festooned with flags, portraits and bunting, as were many private houses. On Coronation Day processions and street parties were held in all parts of the borough. A special event was also held at the Albert Road Recreation Ground to welcome His Royal Highness, Prince Mustapha Ali Bey, Emir of Transjordania, who was in London for the royal event. On arrival he was greeted by a guard of honour comprising members of the British Legion and Fire Brigade. The Emir was particularly impressed by the new open-air swimming pool. It was only after his departure that it was realised the whole thing had been a hoax, known only to a few top civic dignitaries. Two weeks later, a genuine but unscheduled visit to Wood Green was made by Queen Mary, the then Queen Mother, and the Princess Royal. Queen Mary visited the poorer parts of the borough and the best decorated house at 6, Blenheim Road, much to the surprise of local people.

The Coronation of Queen Elizabeth II in 1952 provided the light relief necessary after the war years. Like previous coronation celebrations the day was marred by bad weather but the usual events were held even if delayed for a few days. This was the first coronation with full TV coverage. At that time TV film processing, as well as transmission, was carried out at Alexandra Palace. Press reports describe helicopter landings on the cricket field to bring the film for processing and onward delivery to Canada.

The 25th anniversary celebrations of Wood Green Borough Council were held in 1958. The events included an exhibition of railway rolling stock at Noel Park Goods Yard, a horticultural show, an art exhibition at the Gaumont Palace Cinema, a Thanksgiving Service at St Michael's Church, various parades and sporting events and a performance by massed choirs at Alexandra Palace.

PARLIAMENTARY REPRESENTATION

Only for a brief period was Wood Green a constituency of its own, returning its own MP. Otherwise, it has shared its MP with neighbouring districts.

Until 1885 Middlesex returned only two MPs for the whole county, outside the metropolitan districts. Wood Green voters, restricted to freeholders, were part of the return for Tottenham and few in number. But Tottenham landowners' votes were a factor in the election of radical reformers in the 18th century. Of these the most famous was John Wilkes (1725-97), who despite being elected three times as a Member for Middlesex between 1768 and 1769, was prevented

166. *Spouters Corner. Cartoon by C.E. Simpkins, 1961. Wood Green first became a location for a political meeting called by the Reform League in 1867. By the end of the nineteenth centuy the common land on the southern corner of Lordship Lane and the High Road became a venue for stump orators and political gatherings, thereby acquiring its name of Spouters Corner. Its significance intensified during the First World War and the inter-war years. It had also been an assembly point for contracting local labour before Labour Exchanges were introduced in 1910. In the post-war years it attracted both local and national political figures and saw CND meetings during the late 1950s and 1960s. In more recent years political speakers have favoured the forecourt of the Central Library. Today, Spouters Corner is the location of Wood Green's newest landmark, a multi-screen cinema complex.*

from taking his seat by government skulduggery and imprisonment and was only able to do so in 1774. The like-minded reformer, Sir Francis Burdett, was also strongly supported by the Tottenham vote in his election in 1802.

TOTTENHAM DIVISION (1885-1918)
From 1885 Middlesex returned seven MPs of which Tottenham (including Wood Green) returned one. The division's first MP was a Tottenham-born lawyer, Joseph Howard (1834-1923), a Conservative, until his retirement in 1906. He was succeeded by Percy Alden (1865-1944), a journalist, representing Labour until 1918. Alden had been a West Ham councillor (1892-1901) and went on to be MP for Tottenham (1923-24). He supported women's suffrage which had strong local support. The first meeting of

suffragettes in Tottenham Division took place in Wood Green in March 1907 at the Higher Grade Board School in Bounds Green Road. Percy Alden specialised in labour problems and was knighted in 1933.

WOOD GREEN, SOUTHGATE & FRIERN BARNET (1918-50)
An increased population and an extension of emancipation led to the creation of Wood Green Division in 1918. It also contained Southgate and Friern Barnet. This became a Conservative seat returning Godfrey Locker-Lampson (1875-1946) in all elections from 1918 to 1931. He was a junior minister under Baldwin (1924-29) and Lloyd-George (1929-31), but he retired due to ill-health in 1935. Between 1935 and 1950 the seat was held by Canadian-born Arthur Beverley Baxter (1891-

167. *Mrs Joyce Butler, MP for Wood Green 1955-79*

168. *Reg Race, MP for Wood Green, 1979-83.*

169. *Sir Hugh Rossi, MP for Hornsey & Wood Green, 1983-1990.*

170. *Barbara Roche, MP for Hornsey & Wood Green from 1990.*

1964), a journalist and former editor of the *Daily Express* between 1929-33. He subsequently became MP for Southgate between 1950-64 and was knighted in 1954.

WOOD GREEN CONSTITUENCY (1950-83)

In 1950 the borough of Wood Green became a parliamentary constituency in its own right, as did Southgate and Friern Barnet. It returned a Labour MP for the next 33 years. Between 1950 and 1955 he was William John Irving (1892-1967), a political organiser and Middlesex County councillor, who had previously held Tottenham North (1945-50). He was succeeded in 1955 by Mrs Joyce Butler who held the seat for the next 24 years.

Mrs Butler and her husband, Vic Butler, had been prominent Wood Green councillors. She was Council Leader (1954-55) and Deputy Mayor (1962-63), and while still an MP she was elected Chair of the London Borough of Haringey (1964-65), Mayoress (1965-66) and Alderman (1964-68). She retained the Wood Green seat in 1974, when it became part of the Haringey Division, until her retirement in 1979. She held junior ministerial office in the Wilson government of the 1960s.

Between 1979-83 the seat was held for Labour by Reg Race who was identified with the left wing of the party.

HORNSEY & WOOD GREEN CONSTITUENCY (1983-)

Wood Green's parliamentary independence came to an end in 1983 when the Hornsey and Wood Green constituency came into being. A Conservative solicitor, Sir Hugh Rossi, was returned as MP in 1983 and again in 1987. He had been MP for the Hornsey constituency since 1966, a government whip (1970-74), Minister of State at the Northern Ireland Office (1979-81) and was at Social Security (1981-83) in Mrs Thatcher's government. Sir Hugh also took an active interest in establishing the Alexandra Palace Statutory Advisory Committee in 1981.

By the 1990 General Election Hornsey & Wood Green had become a very marginal seat and Rossi was defeated by Barbara Roche (Labour) who followed in the tradition of previous Wood Green MPs, becoming a junior minister in 1997. She is now a Minister of State in the Home Office.

Wartimes

With the threat of war with France in 1859 a volunteer force was raised by prominent Tottenham residents as the 33rd Middlesex (Tottenham) Volunteer Rifle Corps. This force did not prove popular with Wood Green residents whose lack of support was condemned at Vestry meetings. The unit survived, nevertheless, and was known later as the 3rd Middlesex Rifle Volunteers, becoming a territorial battalion of the Middlesex Regiment in 1907.

THE FIRST WORLD WAR

The First World War was declared on 4 August 1914. Over six thousand Wood Green residents either volunteered or were conscripted between 1914 and 1918, and of these about one thousand lost their lives. Their memorial is in Crescent Gardens, opposite St Michael's Church. Paid for by public subscription, it is made of Portland stone in the form of a Grecian classical altar; it was unveiled on Armistice Day, 11 November 1920 by Godfrey Locker-Lampson MP, when 20,000 people were present. At that time 800 names were inscribed on the memorial but in 1922 a further tablet was added bringing the total to 980 men and 2 women.

Many Wood Green people were witness to the Zeppelin airship and aircraft raids over North London during 1915-18. The Tottenham historian, Fred Fisk, in his *History of Tottenham* (1923), provides an eye-witness account of all the twenty-one air-raids over Tottenham and Wood Green during 1915-18. The following example describing the Cuffley airship incident captures the moment:

> Sept. 3 and 4, 1916. Thirteen Zepps visited England, three got to London, but did not drop bombs. One machine, at least, was heard over Tottenham at midnight, and followed the High Road from Bruce Grove, then turned westward, followed by the concentrated firing of the many powerful guns surrounding Tottenham. Words cannot convey any idea of the deafening noise, or the shaking of houses, or the effect upon the brave, as well as the nervous, of the working of these guns. Suddenly the guns ceased - we were out of danger, and most people, half clad, made for the open air and described to others their experiences. This was about ten past two in the morning.

Shortly after, in a north-westerly direction, lights were moving round a Zepp - no noise reached me, but suddenly a fiery ball appeared in the sky, and it did not take long for it to become a dazzling blaze, which brilliantly lit up Tottenham, and could he seen forty miles distant. Lieut. Robinson and a party in aeroplanes had attacked the monster Zepp and brought it down in flames at Cuffley! Within a few minutes the Tottenham High Road became a sight, because of thousands of pedestrians, and every description of conveyance, wending tbeir way to Cuffley; this continued throughout the day.

No doubt there were similar scenes in Wood Green High Road. Raids by enemy Giant and Gotha bi-planes began in 1917, and local people were witness to the associated dog-fights. The first moonlight raid was on 4 September 1917 and these continued until May of the following year. Fortunately, there were no fatalities and damage in the area was restricted to broken windows, mainly caused by shrapnel from responding anti-aircraft shells.

Alexandra Palace and Park were turned over to the war effort in August 1914 when they were used by the King Edward's Horse Regiment for training and mobilisation. In September of that year they were requisitioned by the Government to temporarily house Belgian refugees who had fled their country in advance of the enemy. Over the next six months some 38,000 refugees passed through. In 1915 the Palace and Park became an internment camp for aliens and by 1916 their number had reached 2334, mainly Germans and Austrians. It was during this period that the

171. The Wood Green War Memorial, Crescent Gardens, High Road. It was unveiled on 14 November 1920.

south slope of the park, used for recreation by the internees, was enclosed by barbed wire. The Palace and Park remained under the control of the War Office until 1920.

Special constables were recruited to compensate for policemen now in the armed forces. In Wood Green fifty volunteers enrolled on the first day of recruitment on 14 August 1914 and a total of 454 had enlisted by the end of the war. The Specials performed guard duties throughout the war at each end of the New Southgate railway tunnel, at the New Southgate gas works and at the New River aqueduct over Pymmes Brook, in order to prevent acts of sabotage. They also did six months' guard duty at Alexandra Palace, when it housed alien internees from October 1914 to March 1915, and they provided assistance at air raids, at the fire station, Cottage Hospital and public shelters, and were required to protect alien property after the sinking of the *S.S. Lusitania* in May 1915, when anti-German feelings ran high.

THE SECOND WORLD WAR (1939-45)

At the outbreak of the war on 3 September 1939 Wood Green's open spaces were quickly converted to the war effort: their metal railings and gates, as well as those in private front gardens, were removed as part of the scrap metal collection campaign. Under the slogan of 'Digging for Victory' many of the parks were transformed into allotments, the larger of these being the New River Playing Fields, the White Hart Lane and Albert Road Recreation Grounds, the Old Johnians Sports Ground in White Hart Lane and the Town Hall Park; over 1000 plots came under cultivation in addition to the established ones. Public trench and surface shelters were erected in the recreation grounds at Albert Road, Noel Park and White Hart Lane, on the playing fields at Perth Road, in Avenue Gardens, Town Hall Park and on Wood Green Common.

The ARP were responsible for distributing 3350 indoor Morrison shelters and 4298 outdoor Anderson shelters, the latter often being used as garden sheds after the war. Emergency feeding stations, later known as British Restaurants, were also set up. There were five of these, located in

172. A barrage balloon on Wood Green Common during the last war.

173. *An Emergency Laundry Service van in the last war.*

174. *Emergency Bath Service at Noel Park.*

Commerce Road, Crescent Road, Mayes Road, Myddleton Road and at Noel Park, and they remained operational up to 1948. Mobile bath and laundry facilities were also provided. The underground stations at Bounds Green, Wood Green and Turnpike Lane were commissioned as public shelters with people sleeping on the platforms, as in many other London tube stations.

Much of the work on the home-front during the war was carried out by women. In Wood Green women councillors, such as Mrs Bolster and Mrs Rycroft, played a key role on the war-time Council committees.

Another war-time initiative involved the raising of funds, through savings bonds and certificates, etc. and through public events, for the war effort, particularly for warships and aircraft. During Warship Week in March 1942 the sum of £458,357 was raised in Wood Green, allowing the borough to adopt a new destroyer, *HMS Wizard*, to replace *HMS Ghurka* which had been lost in action. Similarly, the sum of £5000 was raised towards the cost of a Spitfire fighter air-

Wood Green

Observer

NORTH LONDON OBSERVER SERIES
No. 121 New Series.   SATURDAY, APRIL 4, 1942.   Tel.: STAmford Hill 2913.
ONE PENNY

J. H. Martin & Son
(Tottenham) Ltd.
BUILDERS' MERCHANTS
WEST GREEN ROAD,
TOTTENHAM, N.15
for A.R.P. Requirements, Sand,
Ballast, Bricks, Cement, Roofing
Felt, Wallboard, Sandbags, Water-
proofing Mediums, Fire Extin-
guishers, Black-out Blinds, etc.
**Protectablast For
:   Windows   :**

Prompt Delivery   Tel. BOWes Pk. 1147

GURKHA NOW WOOD GREEN'S SHIP

Final Figure Out Today

WOOD GREEN finished its Warship Week on Saturday with the total standing at £458,357. Further sums still coming in are being added and The Mayor (Alderman E. J. Anderton) will announce the final total from the steps of the Public Library today (Thursday) at 1 p.m.

THUS, DESPITE A WORRYING TIME IN THE MIDDLE OF THE WEEK, WOOD GREEN HAS PASSED ITS TARGET OF £400,000 AND IS ENTITLED TO "ADOPT" THE NEW HMS GURKHA.

Mayoress Kissed the Sailor!

A GRAND Warship Week social was held at St. Mark's Hall, Noel Park (by permission of the vicar) on Saturday, by the Fire Guard of "C" District. The event was organised by Mr. H. Wendon.

The hall was crowded, and among those who paid a visit during the evening were the Mayor (Ald. E. J. Anderton), who pre-

Third Restaurant

175. Results of fund-raising for Wood Green Warship Week in the Wood Green Observer, 4 April 1942.

craft appropriately named *Borough of Wood Green*, which also carried the borough's coat of arms.

Wood Green was involved in 66 air raids during 1940-41 and 1944-45. According to ARP records, a total of 350 incendiary bombs, 142 high explosive, 7 oil bombs, four V1s, ('Flying Bombs') and two V2s (long-range rockets), fell on Wood Green together with 22 anti-aircraft shells; fortunately nineteen of the latter did not explode. Mercifully, there were no parachute bombs (land mines). The first bomb on 25 August 1940 fell on Park Ridings but did not explode and the first (non-fatal) casualties were in Pellatt Grove and Watson's Road on 18 September 1940. The first three fatal casualties were at Barratt's factory on 25 September 1940 and the most serious single incident occurred on 13 October 1940 when a high explosive bomb fell on Bounds Green Underground station penetrating down to the platforms then in use as a public air-raid shelter. Nineteen were killed in the station and over 50 injured. As a result of his efforts to rescue the injured in this incident, Dr Malcolm Manson,

then Wood Green's Medical Officer of Health, was awarded the George Medal.

The V1 and V2 raids of 1944-45 were very destructive, killing 43 and injuring 200. In the early months of 1945 the Noel Park area took the brunt of these attacks with many houses in West Beech Road, Pelham Road, Gladstone Avenue and Farrant Avenue destroyed.

By the end of the war 254 Wood Green service personnel had perished in action or as a result of injuries. Many of these, in common with those from the First World War are commemorated in Allied military cemeteries throughout the world and in local cemeteries. An inscription to their memory was added to the War Memorial and unveiled on Armistice Day, 9 November 1947. A total of 84 civilians lost their lives directly as a result of the air-raids on Wood Green and 300 were wounded; a further 67 residents died as a result of injuries or incidents elsewhere. The names and addresses of Wood Green's civilian dead are commemorated in the nation's Roll of Honour in Westminster Abbey.

Leisure and Pleasure

PRIZE FIGHTING

Perhaps the first spectator sport in Wood Green appeared on 7 January 1805 when a prize-fight, the precursor of professional boxing, took place between Tom Cribb and George ('The Veteran') Maddox. This was Cribb's first public bout for a winner's purse of 20 guineas and he won after 76 rounds and went on to become champion of England and a prize-fighting legend. The sport became popular during the Regency period and

176. Tom Cribb (1781-1848) prize-fighting champion of England depicted in a fight in 1811. He made his debut at Wood Green on 7 January 1805.

found sponsors amongst the nobility, landed gentry and innkeepers. The venues for these bouts, which were illegal, were usually passed by word of mouth and kept secret. Although boxing was regularised by the introduction of the Queensberry Rules in 1867 prize-fighting persisted. *The Standard* of 6 April 1882 reported:

> Prize fight at an early hour on 5th April 1882 in the neighbourhood of Wood Green between two working men Adams and Cook the stakes being £10. The affair took place quietly and no interruption by the police. About 50 persons witnessed the fight, fourteen rounds in 35 minutes. Cook won, both were disfigured.

HORSE RACING

The number of sports possible in the area increased markedly with the creation of Alexandra Park in 1863. Original plans for activities included a cricket ground, archery butts, tennis courts and a horse-racing course.

The first horse race meeting was on 30 June 1868, attracting 40,000 spectators. In the 1920s there were six meetings a year but the number fluctuated with the financial ups and downs of the Palace. They were generally one of the more successful enterprises undertaken by the Trustees and any moral objections were set aside in favour of the income they generated. The five-furlong course was unusual and described variously as a 'tennis racket' or 'frying pan' and a long distance race as 'twice round the pan and once up the handle'. It was the only course where, during certain races the contestants passed the grandstand twice - in different directions! The course came in for criticism from racing commentators and the Jockey Club, the latter insisting in 1913 on modifications. It was the home of the London Cup and from 1955 staged evening meetings. Many of Britain's leading jockeys appeared there but the tricky nature of the course was not always to their liking: Steve Donoghue, champion jockey in 1914, took part in 82 races there but only rode eleven winners, but on the other hand Gordon Richards, champion jockey in 1927, won four out of seven races and the London Cup that year. The racecourse (the only one in Middlesex) survived until 1970 when its licence was withdrawn by the Jockey Club on safety grounds.

177. The first horse-race meeting at Alexandra Park on 30 June 1868. From the Illustrated London News.

PONY TROTTING

Trotting, a novel sport to Britain, was introduced at Alexandra Park in 1875 when the second Palace opened. It took place on a half-mile circuit inside the race-course 'frying pan' and the first meeting attracted 15,000 spectators. Over the next few years attendances were between 8-10,000. The introduction of American rules in 1882 did not prove popular, attendances declined and meetings ceased for several years. In 1886 a new trotting ring was laid out and meetings organised by the Alexandra Park Trotting Club, which controlled the sport in the south of England, thrived. In the early 1890s trotting became the major attraction here with twice as many meetings as for horse-racing, but it was a short-lived success as a result of the formation of the Trotting Union of Great Britain and Ireland whose rules, deriving from the north of England, led to conflict. At the same time the Alexandra Park's trotting entrepreneur retired. After only two meetings in 1894 trotting at Alexandra Park ceased.

CYCLE RACING

The Victorian enthusiasm for cycling also featured in the early plans for the park. A mile-long gravel cycle race track was laid within the race course at Alexandra Park in time for the opening of the second Palace on 1 May 1875. The early machines were penny-farthings, tricycles and even tandem tricycles, all with solid tyres. Big events here included a 50-mile Oxford *vs* Cambridge Bicycling Match in 1876; a five-day Cyclists' Camp at Whitsun, 1884, which attracted a thousand cyclists; a three-day International Cycling Meeting in 1886; and in 1887 a four-day Great Jubilee International Cycling Tournament.

By the 1890s, when the bicycle was similar to today's machine, cycling clubs became popular and a number of purpose-built banked cycle racing tracks were built in the London area. One of these was located within half a mile of the Alexandra Park circuit. The North London Cycling & Athletics Grounds Ltd established its Wood Green track on the 10-acre site of the former Nightingale Hall on the south of Bounds Green Road, adjacent to the former Palace Gates Railway station. This opened on 7 June 1895. The operating company was sponsored by A.W. Gamage, himself a racing cyclist, and proprietor

178. *A Trotting Match at Alexandra Palace. Scenes from The Graphic, 8 November 1879.*

179. Wood Green Cycling Track, Bounds Green Road. Start of 24-hour Professional Race, August 1896.

of the famous Holborn store, who lived nearby at Muswell Hill. The track was designed by Harry J. Swindley of *The Cyclist* magazine and built by J.O. McQuone of Scarborough. It was 500 yards in circumference (3° laps to the mile) made of concrete with 8-foot banking on the bends. A covered grandstand seated 1500 and an uncovered stand seated 300, the remainder standing. Attendances of up to 15,000 were recorded for major events.

Many innovative events were held here. In July 1895 a 24-hour marathon race was held, and on Easter Monday 1896 the first outdoor Ladies' Cycling Race (England *vs* France) in Britain was held as well as a 10-mile paced race for men and a two-mile 'Daisy Race' with mixed pairs on tandems. A frequent visitor was the professional cyclist, Charley Barden, who was National Sprint Champion (1895) and twice second in the World Professional Sprint Championships (1896 and '97). In 1896 Barden took part in a 'Cyclist versus runner' event over 220 yards which were popular at the time.

That year marked the heyday of cycle-track racing at Wood Green, for in five years the site was taken for the development of Braemar, Cornwall and Northcott Avenues.

In November 1902 cycle racing returned to the Alexandra Palace with the opening of the Velodrome, a removeable indoor track 200 feet long and 86 feet wide, laid between the columns of the Great Hall. This was the only indoor track in Europe at that time and 3,500 spectators attended the first meeting. Like the luckless Palace, the Velodrome was shortlived on account of financial problems. The Palace also staged a cycle road racing event in 1937 but this too proved to be a one-off.

ROLLER SKATING

A privately-run removable roller skating rink operated in the north-west concert hall of the Alexandra Palace from 1876. It was taken over by the Trustees in 1907, by which time a permanent rink had been laid. During the 1920s and

'30s roller skating was an extremely popular pastime and proved to be a successful enterprise for the Palace. The Alexandra Park Rink Hockey team was formed and won the London League four times between 1923 and 1927. The speed skating club was very successful in the early 1930s, and some of its members became national champions. During 1935 the rink attracted 70,000 attendances. In 1936 three members of the Alexandra Park Skating Club were selected for the British Olympic roller skating team, one winning Gold in the roller hockey team. The rink was closed in 1974 pending repairs to the roof but was destroyed in the 1980 fire. In the redevelopment plans for the Palace ice-skating took preference over roller skating and an ice-rink was opened in the east wing in July 1990. This has proved popular but is not the weekly mecca that the roller rink was in the early 1970s.

HARRINGAY STADIUM AND ARENA
Within the boundaries of the original Wood Green ward and later only a few minutes' walk from the borough boundary was another major sport-

180. Programme for the bout between Randolph Turpin and Tommy Yarosz, 12 December 1950.

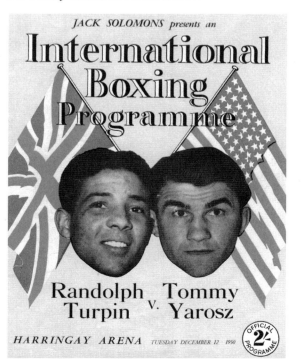

ing venue. The Harringay Stadium, able to accommodate up to 50,000 spectators, was opened in 1927 in Green Lanes on the site of the former Williamson's Pottery. Built by the Greyhound Racing Association, it was one of London's first greyhound racing stadiums. Speedway racing on a dirt track inside the greyhound circuit was introduced in 1929. The home team, the Harringay Racers, were one of the foremost London teams with legendary riders, such as Vic Duggan and Split Waterman, pulling in the crowds, in the '50s and '60s. Speedway ceased in the 1960s to be followed by the rough and tumble of stock-car racing until the stadium was closed in September 1987.

The Harringay Arena, designed by Oscar Faber with a capacity of 11,000, adjacent to the stadium, was opened in 1936 for boxing, ice-skating and ice-hockey. Major boxing fixtures, promoted by Jack Solomons, were held there featuring such boxing greats as Bruce Woodcock, Jack Gardner, Don Cockell, Freddie Mills and Dick and Randolph Turpin. The Harringay Racers ice-hockey team used the ice rink, as did Tom Arnold's Ice Shows. the Arena also staged Tom Arnold's Circus, the American evangelist Billy Graham and the Horse of the Year show.

The Arena was closed in 1958 and its site and that of the stadium were subsequently replaced by warehouse shops such as Sainsbury's.

SPORTS CLUBS AND SOCIETIES
Many of Wood Green's present-day sports clubs date back a century or more when they took advantage of the facilities of Alexandra Park and those of the local authorities.

The Alexandra Park Cricket Club was founded in 1888, its original pitch being on waste ground in Victoria Road, and later on the site of Outram, Clyde and Harcourt Roads before moving to the Racecourse Ground, located within the 'frying pan' in Alexandra Park, in 1906. During the 1920s and '30s the club could claim to be one of the strongest in London. It also claimed to be the first English cricket club to make a tour of France, and was a founder member of the Cricket Club Conference in 1915. The club celebrated its centenary in 1988 and still flourishes today.

The Alexandra Park Football Club was formed in 1889 and made the football field at Alexandra Park, near the lake, its home ground from 1937. The Club distinguished itself in the mid-1950s by winning the Southern Amateur League Championship and the AFA Senior Cup.

181. *Wood Green Town Football Club, 1908-1909.*

The Wood Green Town FC, an amateur club, was established in 1907 with origins in the Tufnell Park FC. By the 1920s it had its own ground on the north side of White Hart Lane. In the post-war years it relocated to a ground on the south side of White Hart Lane adjacent to Fenton Road, now known as Coles Park, where it played in the Spartan and Middlesex Leagues. The club name survived until the late 1970s, later merging with other local teams and today its spirit lives on in the Haringey Borough FC.

Indoor and outdoor bowls clubs were at Alexandra Palace from its early days. The Bounds Green Bowls and Tennis Club, in Brownlow Road, began in 1887 having been a tennis and croquet club two years earlier on the nearby Broomfield Estate. Municipal bowling greens were created at Woodside Park, Albert Road Recreation Ground, Noel Park and Chapmans Green by the beginning of the 20th century. The Glencairn Sports Club in Blake Road was founded in 1924 by E.L. Cole, of Cole's Potteries in White Hart Lane, and continues today.

Tennis courts featured in the first plans for Alexandra Park in 1863. New courts were laid out by the boating lake in 1911, becoming the home of the Avenue Lawn Tennis Club. Additional courts were added near The Grove in 1920. In 1934 three lawn tennis clubs (Alexandra Park, Grove and Hillside) were based at Alexandra Park in addition to those at Bounds Green, Wolves Lane (Oakfield L.T. club) and Rhodes Avenue (Rhovian Tennis Club). In 1935 municipal courts were at the Albert Road, Chapmans Green, Noel Park and White Hart Lane Recreation Grounds and on the New River Playing Fields.

The Muswell Hill Golf Course, established in 1893, occupies the northern part of the old Tottenham Wood Farm. The farmhouse was used as the clubhouse until 1932 when it was demolished except for the portico which still stands today in Rhodes Avenue.

Athletics and gymnastics clubs were formed by some of the churches during the 1880s and '90s. By 1917 the Wood Green Athletics Association, an umbrella group embracing various sections, was in existence and in 1933 this organisation had seventeen different sections. In that year, the athletics section, known as the Harriers, broke away from the main body to become the Southgate Harriers Athletics Club which quickly established a reputation in national and international events before and after the last war. In 1973, the club held its first meeting at the recently built New River Sports Centre. It amalgamated with the Haringey Athletics Club in 1974 and for the next twenty years dominated Division One of the British Athletics League. The club continues today as the Enfield and Haringey AC. The New River Sports Centre became the training ground of many international athletes, including Stan Cox, Heather and Gary Oakes, Sebastian Coe and Daley Thompson to name but a few.

PURSUITS AND PASTIMES

The St James's (Presbyterian Church) Literary Society was founded on 22 September 1880 and survived at least to the outbreak of the last war, and in 1930 the Bowes Park Congregational Church sponsored a Literary and Social Union.

One of the earliest local voluntary organisations for young people was the Band of Mercy movement founded by Mrs Catherine Smithies of Earlham Grove House, in 1857. This encouraged young people to care for animals and birds – similar groups were formed around the country and in the USA. Eventually the Band of Mercy was integrated as a young people's branch of the RSPCA. In a similar vein Wood Green also attracted attention in 1924 with the opening of the Wood Green Animal Shelter for stray and neglected animals at 601 Lordship Lane. In the 1930s the charity grew and could offer treatment and care for animals and by the 1950s additional premises were obtained at Heydon, Hertfordshire and later at Godmanchester, Cambridgeshire and more recently in Worcestershire. The original premises in Lordship Lane remain today offering daily clinic sessions.

Uniformed organisations for young people came into being early in the 20th century to provide activities coupled with a moral and spiritual message. The 1st Bounds Green (later 151st North London) Boy Scout troop was formed in 1908, the year the Boy Scouts movement began, and the Alexandra Park No. 1 Troop (later the 157th North London) was formed the year after at St Saviour's church, Alexandra Park. A St Michael's Scout Troop was founded in 1910 and a Girl Guides company in 1920; both survived until recent amalgamations.

MUSIC HALLS AND THEATRES

The first theatre in Wood Green was the Alexandra Palace Theatre situated in the east wing of the second Palace. It was designed by Grieve with a stage virtually the same size as at the Drury Lane Theatre and seating for 3,000. Its first season had extravagant music hall turns which included performing goats, elephants and high-wire acts. Operas were performed by 1879 and in 1895 the theatre was licensed for stage plays. In 1903 the Alexandra Palace Dramatic Society performed *The Streets of London* which involved the Wood Green Fire Brigade. In the same year Master Vyvian Thomas, the 'boy actor', performed in *Little Lord Fauntleroy* and in 1909, *The Forty Thieves* was staged including acrobatics by the Leopold Brothers. Later that year the theatre's licence was revoked pending improvements but public meetings continued. One, held by the Suffragettes and featuring Mrs Sylvia Pankhurst and Mrs Pethick-Lawrence, had to be abandoned because of interruptions by rowdy

182. Opening of the Wood Green Horticultural Show by Dame Barbara Brooke, 6 September 1963.

183. *Wood Green Salvation Army Sunbeam Brigade, c.1937.*

184. *Wood Green Young People's Band, 1930.*

185. Wood Green's prize-winning Choir, 1909.

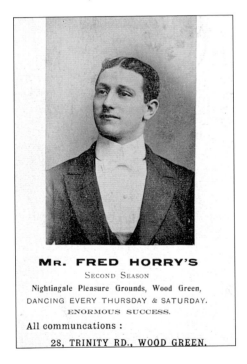

MR. FRED HORRY'S
SECOND SEASON

Nightingale Pleasure Grounds, Wood Green,
DANCING EVERY THURSDAY & SATURDAY.
ENORMOUS SUCCESS.

All communcations :

28, TRINITY RD., WOOD GREEN.

186. Advertising card for Fred Horry (who lived in Trinity Road) for his appearances at the Nightingale Pleasure Grounds, 1906.

youths. In 1911 performances resumed with works by the Finchley Operatic Society and the theatre was also used as a cinema as a result of which it realised a profit for the first time. The theatre was refurbished in 1922 with improved seating and accessibility and it benefited from programming by W. MacQueen Pope who was then general manager. The renewed theatre saw *Cinderella* in pantomine, a series of London plays, opera, and a season by the Alexandra Park Amateur Dramatic Society, as well as by other local societies during the late 1920s. The theatre never reopened after the last war, and suffered from neglect thereafter. Although plans were proposed for remedial work and use as a recording studio, these were thwarted by the 1980 fire, after which plans for its future have not been realised.

THE WOOD GREEN EMPIRE
Wood Green's theatre-goers had the choice of the Crouch End Hippodrome (from 1897) and the Palace of Varieties at Tottenham (from 1908), but on 9 September 1912, the Wood Green Empire, designed by Frank Matcham for Oswald Stoll, was built on the High Road as part of the Noel Park development. The Empire, with a 43 foot stage, offered 'a theatre of varieties in opera,

concert, circus, music hall and cinemas'.

Early performers included music hall artistes Ella Shield, G.H. Elliott, Joe Elwin, Will Evans, George Lockwood, Gertie Gitana and Vesta Tilley, and actors Seymour Hicks, Ellaline Terriss, Lilian Braithwaite, Gladys Cooper and Edmund Glenn. In the 1930s performers included Florence Desmond, Cyril Fletcher, Ronald Frankau, Tommy Handley, Leslie ('Hutch') Hutchinson, Leon Cortez, Billy Russell, Bebe Daniels and Ben Lyon, and Sid Field. There were visiting bands such as those of Joe Loss, Maurice Winnick, Harry Roy and Henry Hall. Musical comedies included *The Belle of New York*, *The Chocolate Soldier* and *The Desert Song*. During the last war Vera Lynn, Suzette Tarri, Ann Shelton, Jack Train, Issy Bonn, Hal Bowly and Max Miller all appeared there. After the war there were musicals such as *The White Horse Inn*, *King's Rhapsody*, *Bless the Bride*, *The Song of Norway*, and individual artists such as Winifred Atwell, Dorothy Squires, Alma Cogan and Shirley Bassey. Local performers included Macari and his accordion band and the Western Brothers.

The Empire also acquired a tragic reputation over the years. On 23 March 1918 the illusionist 'Chung Ling Soo' (William Elsworth Robinson) was killed during his act of catching 'live bullets' fired from a rifle and twelve years later a patron

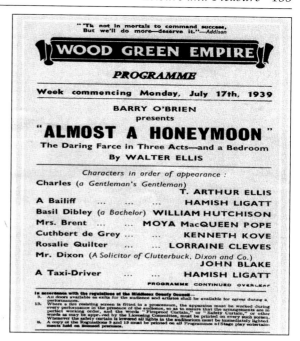

188. Wood Green Empire programme, 1939.

committed suicide in the auditorium. In 1939 another illusionist, Horace Goldin, died after only one performance at the Empire.

Audiences fell in the post-war years and the building was neglected, so much so that its licence was not renewed. The last performance was on 31 January 1955 after a run of *Cinderella*.

The building was used during the late 1950s and early '60s by Associated Television as a production studio. Here were initiated such programmes as *Emergency Ward 10* and *Probation Officer*. ATV left the Empire in 1963 after which it was closed. The Empire's facade remains above the Halifax Building Society office in the High Road but the auditorium became the site for a Sainsbury's supermarket.

CINEMAS

Wood Green has a rich heritage of cinemas. Some were in existence by 1910 and by the end of the 1930s seven were operating within the borough and a further four were within yards of its southern boundary. Yet by 1992 there were none, although soon there is planned to be at least two multi-screen cinema complexes.

Three cinemas opened in 1910. Probably the first, the Wood Green Electric Theatre, was a converted shop at no.16 High Road, on the corner

187. Wood Green Empire, c.1950.

with Whymark Avenue. By 1912 it was known as the Crown Picture Palace. It had closed down by 1925. Claimed to be the oldest surviving purpose-built cinema in London, the New Curzon, in Frobisher Road facing Ducketts Common, just within the former Hornsey boundary, was opened as the Premier Electric Theatre on 16 April 1910 with seating for 900. It was revamped in 1939 in art-deco style with 690 seats and renamed the Regal, operated by Gaywood Cinemas, and twenty years later became part of the Essoldo circuit. In 1963 the building became a short-lived bingo club but reopened in 1964 as the Curzon cinema. By the early 1980s it offered a diet of sex films during the week and Asian films on Sundays but closed again in 1989. Between 1991-95 it was a laser games venue and briefly used by the Church of Destiny in 1996. It was then taken over by an Indian proprietor who refurbished it to modern cinema standards with 498 seats and re-opened as The New Curzon in October 1997 offering only Indian films.

Another purpose-built cinema, the Cinematograph Theatre, in Lordship Lane, was also opened in 1910 but had closed by the late 1920s. The building became Garner's furniture depository in the 1930s and housed Harry Boult's School of Dancing on the first floor, and in more recent years was an indoor market hall. By a strange irony the building was demolished at the beginning of 1999 to make way for the new six-screen multiplex cinema.

Two cinemas were in Station Road. The Electric Cinema opened in 1914, its entrance squeezed in the space of a shop front at no.18. It became the Palais de Luxe Picture Theatre in 1915 with 796 seats and was reconstructed in 1931 by Gaywood Cinemas. In 1946 it was known as the Rex and was taken over by Essoldo in 1950. It ceased to function as a cinema in 1964 re-opening as a bingo club later that year. It survived a few years before being demolished in the mid-70s' redevelopment. The site of the auditorium is now the car-park adjacent to Alexandra House.

The Central Cinema Theatre at 35 Station Road was opened around 1915 and stood on the eastern corner of Brabant Road. This 825-seat cinema remained open until the last war after which it became a warehouse and was later demolished to make way for a council office block in the 1960s redevelopment.

The Palladium Cinema at 46 High Road existed in 1914, probably occupying a shop. It later

189. *The Premier Electric Cinema in Frobisher Road, April 1910, the year of its opening. This is claimed to be the oldest surviving purpose-built cinema in London.*

became known as the Wood Green Picture Palladium and closed in 1934, the site being taken over by Marks & Spencer.

Wood Green's most prestigious cinema, the Gaumont Palace, in The Broadway, High Road, was opened on 26 March 1934. It was designed by W.E. Trent and Ernest F. Tulley, in art-deco style said to be influenced by the former Titania-Palast cinema in Berlin, and could seat over 2500. The building features a huge semi-circular proscenium arch and impressive entrance hall and foyer and the safety curtain has the signs of the zodiac painted by Frank Barnes. By 1954 it had become the Gaumont and in 1962 it was renamed Odeon. The organ was removed in 1966 and is now at Thorngate Hall, Gosport. In 1973 the cinema was converted to three screens, totalling 1113 seats. A 170-seat restaurant which once occupied the first floor became the Avenida banqueting suite in the '70s and later a dance studio. The Odeon closed on 7 January 1984 and was converted by Top Rank for bingo but the basic fabric of the building and some of its original features were restored. As a consequence the building was Grade II listed in 1990. The original name Gaumont Palace was restored to the front of the building in 1993. The bingo club closed in July 1996 and the building has remained closed since then. At the time of writing there are proposals for it to be taken over by the Universal Church of God. In view of the importance of this building in the history of cinema architecture, English Heritage recommended its upgrading to Grade II* at the end of 1999.

190. Cinematograph Theatre, Lordship Lane, 1913. It was built in 1910 and closed in the 1920s.

Three other cinemas were situated within the boundary of the original Wood Green ward. The earliest was the Coliseum in Green Lanes (corner of St Ann's Road) opened as the Electric Coliseum in 1910, seating 641. It was the only independent cinema in the area and closed in 1963 to become a bingo club and later a furniture store. It remains derelict pending redevelopment.

The Imperial Theatre at 290-4 West Green Road was opened on 6 November 1913 seating 550. Originally operated by the Lion Cinematograph Co., it was in the hands of Mayfair Ltd in 1944 and became an Essoldo in 1949. Closed in 1958 it remains today as a discount carpet store.

The Coronet, Turnpike Parade, Green Lanes was the most recent cinema to disappear (in August 1999) to make way for redevelopment of the Turnpike Lane bus station. It began as the Ritz, operated by ABC, in December 1935, being part of an art-deco shopping parade adjacent to the new Turnpike Lane Underground station. Renamed ABC in 1961, it was converted to a three-screen cinema in 1977. It was acquired by Cannon in 1986 and renamed likewise and then taken over by Coronet and thus renamed again in 1988. The cinema closed in May 1999 and was demolished later that year to make way for an extension of the bus garage.

191. The art-deco interior of the Gaumont Palace.

Some Personalities

Many people who have influenced the development of Wood Green have been described in earlier chapters. Others have become prominent in the arts, business, politics and science.

Early local industrialists and tradesmen, such as the proprietors of Cole's and South's potteries and Barratt's confectioners, also took an active part in local politics or community life. Sydney Brandon Cole JP, Wood Green mayor in 1934, is now commemorated by Coles Field, home of the Haringey Borough FC. Samuel South made his contribution via the local Rotary Club.

There were several prominent female politicians in the 20th century. Mrs J.J. Bolster was the first woman councillor to be elected to the Wood Green UDC in 1919 and became Wood Green's first woman mayor in 1938-39. She will also be remembered for forming the Wood Green Old Folks' Club – it was the first of its kind in the country. Mrs Joyce Butler, Wood Green's MP for 24 years (1955-79) was also an unstinting local councillor (1947-64) and mayor (1962-63). She was described as a feminist before the term was commonplace, pioneering the Women's Cervical Cancer campaign and promoting women's rights and, in good Wood Green tradition, opposed cruelty to animals.

Dr Edith Summerskill (1901-1980), the anti-boxing campaigner, spent her formative years as a GP and a Middlesex County councillor in the Harringay district. She became Labour MP for West Fulham (1938-55) and then Warrington (1955-61). She was Minister of National Insurance (1951-52) and was created a Life Peer in 1961.

The distinguished film actor, Jack Hawkins (1910-73) was born in Wood Green and attended Trinity County school. From the same school came the actor James Grout, the TV and stage producer Jack Good. The comedian and scriptwriter, Barry Took lived locally. The comedian Tony Hancock (1924-68) lived for a time in Natal Road, Bounds Green. Mike Leigh, the dramatist, theatre, TV and film director also has Wood Green connections. Indeed, in one of his many award-winning films, *Bleak Moments* (1970), there is a brief sequence filmed in Wood Green School, White Hart Lane.

Of writers, perhaps the most famous is Arthur

192. *Alderman Mrs J.J. Bolster, first woman to become mayor of Wood Green (1938-39).*

C. Clarke, the prolific science fiction author and one time resident of Nightingale Road. Another, the Tottenham-born Labour politician, Lord Ted Willis, provides a colourful account of his times in West Green in *Whatever happened to Tom Mix*. One of Wood Green's earlier MPs, Godfrey Locker-Lampson, was also an established author whose many works included *The Country Gentleman and Other Essays* (1932) and *The Disappearance of the English Country Squire* (1946).

Local characters could justify a book of their own. One, Fred Clarke, brother of Arthur C. Clarke, lived and worked in Wood Green before retiring to Somerset. He worked for many years for the local heating firm of Hobbs Wilson Ltd, was an active member of the Ratepayers' Association and was involved in youth and community work. He was also involved with Alexandra Palace and particularly the Willis Organ Fund. He provides some amusing anecdotes of his Wood Green years in his book *Alexandra Palace & People* (1995).

Postscript

The boroughs of Wood Green, Hornsey and Tottenham were merged to form the London Borough of Haringey in 1965. The coat of arms of the new Borough includes radiating golden rays symbolising action reaching out to the boundaries of the borough; they are also said to allude to the first television transmission from Alexandra Palace – at least an indirect reference to the Wood Green area.

Wood Green's location at the geographical centre of the new borough was to be significant. The former Wood Green Civic Centre became the Haringey Civic Centre after the creation of the new borough. And in the mid-1970s the Greater London Council's development plans envisaged Wood Green as one of London's strategic centres and local plans proposed it as the 'Town Centre' of Haringey.

Redevelopment of the New River Playing Fields had been initiated by Wood Green Borough Council and was continued by the new authority, leading to the opening of the New River Sports Centre, serving the whole borough in 1975.

The early 1970s also saw more redevelopment of the central area. Many of the remaining older properties in Station Road were replaced by office blocks, encouraged by the GLC's office relocation initiative and the proximity of good transport connections. This led to the demolition in 1973 of the original and distinctive Wood Green Library, which was replaced by River Park House in 1975. Another casualty was the mock Tudor House, built in 1925, housing a multitude of small businesses, which was replaced by the Education Services offices.

Closure of the old LNER Palace Gates branch railway line in 1963 released substantial land in the central area. This enabled the development of Shopping City (*see* p103), the Central Library, the Sandlings housing development on the Noel Park goods yard, and the Middlesex University hostel in Brabant Road. Refurbishment and extenson of the Shopping City began in 1999 to incorporate a 12-screen cinema complex.

The area contained within Coburg, Mayes and Western Roads was designated as a light industrial area attracting new businesses to the area during the 1980s and 1990s. Some of the former Barratt buildings became the Chocolate Factory, defined as a cultural enterprise centre combin-

193. Haringey's coat of arms.

ing creative and business activity. In 1999, the area was re-designated as the 'Haringey Heartlands' with a proposed £130m scheme to create the town centre envisaged in earlier plans. This includes a new campus for Middlesex University, a new Mountview Theatre School and theatre, a hotel with conference and leisure facilities, housing, shops, cafes and galleries. The remaining Wood Green Common, the original heart of Wood Green, will be redesigned and become an integral part of the scheme.

The site of the former Masonic Boys' School in Lordship Lane, was acquired by Haringey council in 1974. The existing building was modernised and became Wood Green Crown Court, opened in 1989. The remainder of the site became housing. Wood Green High Road itself was the subject of a £3m refurbishment scheme completed at the end of 1999.

The cultural identity of Wood Green began to change in the late 1950s with immigrants from the West Indies and then Cyprus, the latter concentrated in the Harringay area. Their numbers were expanded following the Turkish invasion of Cyprus in 1974. Immigrants of Indian origin followed after the excesses of Idi Amin's regime in Uganda in the late 1970s. At the present time over 160 languages and dialects are spoken by Haringey's schoolchildren.

Published Sources

HHS: *Hornsey Historical Society*
EHHS: *Edmonton Hundred Historical Society*

General

Victoria County History, Middlesex, Volume V (1974).
History and Antiquities of Tottenham, William Robinson, 2nd edn. (1840).
History and Antiquities of Tottenham High Cross, Richard Dyson (1790).
History of Tottenham, Fred Fisk (1st series 1913, 2nd series 1923).
The Outer Circle, Thomas Burke (1921).
Ancient Tottenham, William J. Roe (1949).
Tottenham, Edmonton & Enfield Historical Note Book, William J. Roe (1952).
In Times Past - Wood Green and Tottenham with West Green and Harringay, (HHS 1991).
Tottenham, Hornsey and Wood Green, Chris Potz (Haringey Council 1999).
Haringey Before our Time, Ian Murray (HHS 1993)
Kelly's Post Office Directories.

Medieval Estates and Large Houses

Lost Houses of Haringey, (Haringey Community Information / HHS 1986)
People and Places: Lost estates of Highgate, Hornsey and Wood Green, ed. Joan Schwitzer (HHS 1996)

New River

Romance of the New River (New River Co. Annual Report, 1926)
Exploring the New River, Michael Essex Lopresti (1986)

Highways

Drovers and Tanners of Enfield and Edmonton, EHHS Occasional Paper No.51, 19.
History of Enfield, Vols 1 and 2, David Pam.

Farms

Land Use Map of London & Environs in 1800 by Thomas Milne, with explanatory text.   London Topographical Society Publication Nos.118/9.

Railways

Rails to the People's Palace, Reg Davies (HHS, 1980).
Finsbury Park to Alexandra Palace, J.E. Connor (Middleton Press, 1997)
North Woolwich to Palace Gates - A Photographic Journey, J.E. Connor (Connor & Butler, 1997).

Residential Development

Surburban Houses of London - a residential guide, William Spencer Clarke (1881).
Semi-Detached London, by Alan. A. Jackson (1973).
The Middle Classes 1900-1950, Alan A. Jackson (1991)

Churches

Religious Life of London, Richard Maudie-Smith (1903).
St Michael's - A record of One Hundred Years of Life and Work 1844-1944, H.C. Pearcy (1954).
History of St Michael's Church, Wood Green 1844-1994, Fr. Christopher Vipers (1994).
Living Stones - the story of Westbury Avenue Baptist Church, David Rushworth Smith (1981).
St Saviour's Church - Fifty Years of Progress, ed. H. W. de B. Peters (1950).
The History of St Andrew's Church 1899-1950, H.E. Boisseau (1950).

Schools

Some Reflections on Education in Tottenham over the past Three Centuries, H.G. Hawkes. *EHHS Occasional Paper 53,* 1993.
Schools of the Edmonton Hundred, G.W. Sturgess.
Trinity - A School with a Past, ed. Don Grammer (1999)

Almshouses

The Almshouses of London, Clive Berridge (1987).
Almshouses, Brian Bailey (1988).

Shopping

Over the Counter, F.E. Butler and D. Hoy. *EHHS Occasional Paper No.49*

Alexandra Palace and Park

Alexandra Palace & Park - A History, Ron Carrington. (Greater London Council, 1975).
A Palace on the Hill, Ken Gay (HHS, 1992).
Alexandra Palace 1875-1975 - Centenary Programme, pub. by *Illustrated London News.*
Alexandra Palace - Haringey Council's Development Plans, October 1979
Alexandra Palace & Park, Peter Smith. *HHS Bulletin No.24,* 1982

Stage & Screen

Empires, Hippodromes and Palaces, Jack Reid (1985).
Picture House (Magazine of the Cinema Theatre Association) No. 24, Autumn 1999.

Transport

History of London Transport, by T.C. Barker and R. Michael Robbins, Vols I and II, 1963 and 1974.
Roads and Rails of London (1900-1933), Charles F. Klapper (1976).
Golden Age of Buses, Charles F. Klapper (1978).
London Buses, Vol I, The Independent Era (1922-33), Blacker, Lunn and Westgate. HJ Publications, 1977.
LT Bus Garages since 1948, J. Joyce (1988).
Source Book of London Transport, John R. Day (1982).
Enfield & Wood Green Tramways, Dave Jones (1997).

INDEX
Asterisks denote
illustrations or
captions